# Collaborating for Real Literacy: Librarian, Teacher, and Principal

Sharon M. Pitcher, Ed.D.
Bonnie Mackey, Ph.D

**Your Trusted
Library-to-Classroom Connection.
Books, Magazines, and Online**

Library of Congress Cataloging-in-Publication Data

Pitcher, Sharon M.
  Collaborating for real literacy : librarian, teacher, and principal /
Sharon M. Pitcher, Bonnie Mackey.
      p. cm.
  ISBN 1-58683-144-5 (pbk.)
  1.  Reading (Elementary)--United States. 2.  Teaching teams--United
States.  I. Mackey, Bonnie. II. Title.
LB1573.P597 2003
372.4--dc22

                          2003023710



Published by Linworth Publishing, Inc.
480 East Wilson Bridge Road, Suite L
Worthington, Ohio 43085

ISBN: 1-58683-144-5

5 4 3 2 1

# Table of Contents

# Table of Figures

# Dedication

To my daughter
Amy Pitcher
whose literacy journey taught me so much.
I celebrate the literate adult she has become.
And to my husband, Mike,
who supports my literacy passion in so many ways.
*Sharon Pitcher*


To my Daddy
who taught me to read in that faded blue armchair
and
to my Mama
who taught me that flowers blossom with love and hard work.
*Bonnie Mackey*

# Acknowledgments

In writing this book, we realized the power and the direction that elementary librarians, teachers, and principals share as they mold and shape the citizens of tomorrow. It is to them that we graciously acknowledge all that we know and all that we are.

We would like to additionally thank our editor, Donna Miller, and our editorial consultant, Sherry York, for influencing our understanding of the publishing process. Without their insights, this book would not exist.

Finally, we would like to thank our families and friends who supported us throughout the many hours we worked on this, our first book: Sharon's husband, Mike, and daughter, Amy; Sharon's parents, Marge and Norm Sparks (yes, Mom, it is done now); and Bonnie's children (Jenny, Shannon, and Peter). We also appreciate our friends Lauren and Jeff Behar, Bette Hobner, Debra Osborne-Sigrist, and Hans Olsen.

# About the Authors

Sharon M. Pitcher is an Assistant Professor and Director of the Reading Clinic at Towson University in Maryland. Prior to coming to Towson University, she was a reading specialist for 20 years in public and parochial schools in Maryland and has taught reading to all ages from kindergartners to adults. Additionally, she supervised family literacy and adult literacy programs. Dr. Pitcher has her Doctorate in

Education from the University of Maryland and her Master's Degree in Reading from Towson University. Presently, she conducts literacy professional development for administrators and faculties in Baltimore City's CEO's District. Her research interests, which are all focused on literacy, include parent involvement, reading intervention, adolescent literacy, and literacy leadership.

Bonnie Mackey is an Assistant Professor in Early Childhood Education at the University of Houston-Clear Lake in southeastern Texas. She received her Master's Degree in Educational Administration from the University of Texas at El Paso and her Ph.D. in Curriculum and Instruction from Texas A & M University in College Station. Her prior teaching experiences include 13 years in preschool through third grade at both public and private schools. Presently, she serves as the Director of Research for the McWhirter Professional Development Lab School, an innovative partnership between the University of Houston-Clear Lake and Clear Creek Independent School District. Her research interests focus on emergent literacy, student choices of text genres, and the influence of the principal in elementary literacy programs.

# Introduction

The authors of this book define ***real literacy*** as literacy skills and strategies that are explicitly taught to children, who in turn can independently use these skills in their everyday lives. Children will naturally apply these strategies when taking any kind of assessment. Real literacy skills produce higher test scores and real, long-sustained student achievement (Allington, 2001).

The purpose of this book is to suggest collaborative ways that school librarians, teachers, and principals can initiate and sustain a literacy focus within their schools. The authors support whole school efforts to make real literacy and student achievement the focus of instruction, school budgets, and faculty energy. Money spent on quality children's books becomes an investment in the future of the children attending a school for generations. Energy directed towards professional development that involves collaborative efforts of every faculty and staff member pays off in higher teacher retention and increased student achievement. Research supports the link between increased student achievement and quality professional development of faculty and staff. Increased student achievement is also associated with a rich literacy environment that abounds with quality books and materials (Allington, 2001; National Reading Panel, 2000; Snow, Burns, & Griffin, 1998).

Collaboration requires that all partners in the school use the energy and talents of everyone in their learning community to support a unified effort. Administrators sometimes overlook the natural literacy leadership of the school librarian. Who better to find the best books and oversee the infusion of literacy materials in the school and into the classrooms than the school librarian? In an International Reading Association Board Resolution (2000), this body of literacy experts suggests that "credentialed school library media professionals promote, inspire, and guide students towards a love of reading, a quest for knowledge, and a thirst for lifelong learning." Lifelong learning is what "real literacy" is all about. Librarians provide literacy coordination and support that can make a big difference in changing the literacy focus of a school. Our book depicts many practical examples of how librarians can do that.

The U.S. Department of Education (2003) has focused much attention on the importance of research-based instruction in all classrooms. Our book suggests many practical methods to share research and practice with librarians and teachers.

The family's role in this collaboration has also been proven to be essential (National Reading Panel, 2000; Snow, Burns, & Griffin, 1998) so a chapter of the book is devoted to ways to include all school families in this journey towards real literacy. The ideas in this chapter are practical, inexpensive, and designed to include families of all educational and socioeconomic levels.

## Organization of the Chapters

Each chapter begins with a quote (An Educator's Voice) from an educator with whom one of us has worked. The chapter then asks questions that build upon the knowledge base that librarians and teachers have (Anticipation Questions), and extends that knowledge by examining one of the major components that compose real literacy instruction (Exploring the Theory), and is completed with how that theory looks in practice (The Practice). The section titled "The Practice" includes many references to professional books and Internet sites to give the reader access to a handy, well-organized literacy resource. In addition, some of the chapters include a compilation of children's books (Good Books) that provides librarians and teachers with literature to support the instruction of the theory-based practice.

The second half of each chapter is devoted to sections geared to specific instructional leaders in the school. Within the section called "Professional Development Ideas," many ideas for effective professional development practices are offered for yearlong staff development of all the educators in the school. The next section (The Librarian's Link) provides ideas for the librarian to connect library resources, literacy instruction, and leadership efforts. Next, each chapter includes practical suggestions for administrators (The Principal's Perspective) to enable them to collaborate with librarians and teachers to develop literacy leaders within the school. Each chapter ends with a summative vision (The Collaboration) of how the collaboration among librarians, teachers, and principals can look in various schools. A reference section (Reading the Minds of Others), lists books cited and additional readings.

# Suggested Uses of Our Book

This book is a resource for all literacy stakeholders in a school. For librarians, ideas and practical examples are provided to engage you in a collaborative effort with teachers, with families, and with students. For instructional leaders, our book will enable you to transform all rooms in your building to welcoming places where all children receive the literacy support they need. For teachers, we invite you to experience a transformation from working too hard without results to facilitating a classroom where literacy is reached for, celebrated, and enjoyed even by you. For preservice and inservice teachers who are students in undergraduate and graduate library science and literacy courses, this book will provide a view of collaboration among librarians, teachers, and principals.

# References

Allington, R. (2001). *What really matters for struggling readers: Developing research-based programs*. New York: Addison-Wesley Educational Publishers, Inc.

International Reading Association. (2002). *What is evidence-based reading instruction?* Newark, DL: International Reading Association.

International Reading Association. (2000). In support of credentialed library media professionals in school library media centers. Retrieved May 26, 2003, from <http://www.reading.org/positions/cre_libra.html>.

National Reading Panel. (2000). *Teaching children to read: An evidence-based assessment of the scientific research literature on reading and its implications for reading instruction*. Washington, DC: National Institute of Child Health and Human Development.

Snow, C. E., Burns, M. S., & Griffin, P. (Eds.). (1998). *Preventing reading difficulties in young children*. Washington, DC: National Academy Press

United States Department of Education. (2003). *No child left behind*. Retrieved May 30, 2003, from <http://www.nclb.gov>.

# Chapter 1

# Real Literacy in Schools

## An Educator's Voice

"Encouraging people to develop real skills and transfer them to their lives is at the heart of literacy. Real literacy equals independence."

　　Librarian, McWhirter Professional Development Lab School, Houston, Texas

## Anticipation Questions

Although most educators would definitely place a high value on the pursuit of literacy, do their decisions focus on developing this literacy in the children in their schools? Before reading this chapter, consider how you define literacy, and how your decisionmaking influences the way you bring literacy into the lives of students.

　　What is your definition of literacy?
　　What does a literacy-focused school look like?

*As you read, consider how your answers to these questions are changed or are confirmed.*

## Exploring the Theory

Questions like these have forced educators to look at their schools in a different way as national test scores indicate there are large achievement gaps among children of different socioeconomic backgrounds. Ramsey (1997, p. 699) suggests:

> The one thing we know about the future that our young people will live in is that it will be ruled by political, cultural, and technological changes. If we send them into that world unable to inform themselves about people, ideas, ways of life, occupations, and values outside of their own experience they will be overwhelmed and left behind. Even though our young people will have to be much more adept at information management than we are, reading will remain the most powerful, efficient, in-depth, and balanced way of gathering, sorting, and understanding that information

As we widen our lens to what we are teaching and why we are teaching it in schools, we have to start by understanding why we do what we do. "Literate practices are not typically invented by their practitioners" (Brandt & Clinton, 2002, p. 337) but emerge from the culture in which they live. The real demands of our world require "reading, writing, listening, and speaking as well as the social and political influences inherent in literacy processes" (Readence & Barone, 1996, p. 8).

What it means to be literate has evolved by the needs of living in a world of words: words in our everyday environment, words on computers, and words over all airways. Children today, in order to live and achieve in the world of tomorrow, need to be able to use words to read, write, speak, and listen. Our focus in school libraries and classrooms should be on developing literate children who competently use words and are engaged in real literacy activities that will lead them to become literate adults in the literate world.

Strickland (1999, p. xix) suggests that "Becoming literate requires experiences that help make the meaning and importance of print transparent." These experiences need to occur in our schools from the moment that children walk in the door because developing literate children is our most important job. Children need to "follow their own interests, to make connections, to reformulate ideas, and to reach unique conclusions" (Gould, 1996, p. 93). Therefore, how librarians, teachers, and principals collaborate in a literacy-focused school is more about the process of guiding the child to independent application of literacy than about delivering an established content-driven curriculum. This new trend in education focuses on children individually meeting standards of what they will need to know and do to live in our literate world.

Consequently, cognitive theorists who have suggested ways to scaffold the child to independent practice have emerged at the forefront of the movement. Piaget contended that the aim of schools should not be just to instruct children but to support their development, to not furnish the mind but to lead it to respond on its own (DeVries & Kohlberg, 1987). Vygotsky built on Piaget's work and recommended that this journey to responding ideally would occur in a person's "zone of proximal development (ZPD)." Vygotsky defined ZPD as "the distance between the actual developmental level as determined by independent problem solving and the level of potential development as determined through problem solving under adult guidance or in collaboration with more capable peers" (1978, p. 86).

Therefore, the optimal environment for this literacy development to take place is one where strategies for literacy are explicitly taught at the level needed by the learners and then the learners are given the opportunity to see how the strategies apply to their lives. To execute this continuum, the students need to be engaged in reading. Research at the National Reading Research Center in the '90s found that in order to be engaged, the reader needed to be motivated, knowledgeable, and socially interactive (Gambrell, 1996). Guthrie's research suggests that "Engagement and achievement are reciprocal. Students need them both and, in our view, so do teachers and schools" (1997, p. 3).

Gambrell (1996) recommends that this environment for engaged readers include large, well-stocked school libraries, book-rich classrooms, choices, social interaction, opportunities to read lots of books, and appropriate reading incentives.

Staton (1998) suggests that school librarians have recognized the importance of motivation to reading engagement. Her suggestions include all of Gambrell's ideas. In addition, she also recommends reading aloud, talking about books, involving families, encouraging students to take responsibility for one another's learning, and making reading time a reward.

In school-wide literacy programs that use this research as their core, some characteristics are integral:

**1** Literacy is viewed comprehensively, involving reading, writing, listening, and speaking.

**2** Books and reading are the *heart* of the program. Children have access to a well-stocked school library and books in their classrooms.

**3** Skills and strategies are taught both directly and indirectly.

**4** Reading instruction involves learning word recognition and identification, vocabulary, and comprehension.

**5** Writing instruction involves learning to express meaningful ideas and use conventional spelling, grammar, and punctuation to express those ideas.

**6** Students use reading and writing as *tools* for learning in the content areas.

**7** The *goal* of the literacy program is to develop lifelong readers and writers (Tompkins, 2001, p. 37).

Bell even suggests that, "In schools that have closed or eliminated the achievement gap, teachers have a basic commitment to read" (2003, p. 33). His recommendations for what a school needs to do to eliminate this "achievement gap" also include suggestions made by Gambrell, Staton, & Tompkins:

■ The literacy program needs to be school-wide with engagement apparent in every classroom.

■ An atmosphere needs to be developed where students support one another's reading efforts.

■ Teachers, themselves, read. He suggests that teachers should read 10–12 books a year.

■ Books that motivate and spark immediate interest are available to students.

■ All children are taught the higher-level reading strategies (making connections, questioning, visualizing, inferring, analyzing, and synthesizing).

■ Teachers routinely re-teach strategies until students apply them independently.

■ Teachers maintain a checklist of the reading levels of all the children in their classes.

Lance & Loertscher (2003) summarize research done with 3,300 schools since 2000 demonstrating that 10–20 percent increases in student achievement can be directly linked to school literacy collaboration that includes the following:

■ Increasing the number of school librarians that work directly with teachers to buy and oversee the use of books and literacy materials throughout the school,

- Acquiring information technology that can be used in classrooms and in the homes,
- Sustaining budgets that consider high quality literacy materials (both print and electronic) as priorities, and
- Prioritizing opportunities for school librarians and teachers to collaborate in creating quality literacy activities throughout the school and to promote the love of reading.

Kreshen (1993) and McQuillan (1998) share evidence from 100 years of research that suggests that student achievement is directly linked to the amount and quality of books that surround children and teens in school. This research and research done by Allington (2001) give evidence for a close correlation between the amount of time children read and achievement scores. The more children read, the higher their achievement scores.

Therefore, the key to higher student achievement suggested by research and demanded by new federal laws is not expensive reading series and special programs that publishers try to convince administrators that they need. Literacy and student achievement in schools will increase when the following conditions are met:

- A large, rotating collection of high interest books and literacy materials exists in schools.
- Children are given more time to read.
- Collaboration between teachers and school librarians allow for more dynamic planning of school-wide and classroom-based literacy learning.
- More books are available to be lent out to the home.

Many educators realize how important a thriving school library is to supporting real literacy in a school. Although an elementary school library occupies only a small percentage of a school's total physical space, it serves 100 percent of the students and teachers, in addition to the uncounted parents and local neighbors. The Robin Hood Foundation, a private charity, recognized the role of the library as the centerpiece of the school and designated large sums of money to all 656 elementary school libraries in New York City's Public School System. Integral to receiving this aid was the formation of a library advisory board, composed of the school librarian, principal, teachers, parents, the local public librarian, and often officials from nearby museums, zoos, and so forth. Librarians receive training in curriculum collaboration to work with teachers to integrate library resources within the academic agenda. Since the redesign of its library, Clara Barton Elementary School in south Bronx has seen its standardized test scores rise (Lau, 2002).

Unfortunately though, most libraries do not receive these large sums of money given by the Robin Hood Foundation to develop the school library as the centerpiece of the school literacy program. However, Teale (1999) suggests that all school libraries can begin to create this centerpiece by following three cost-effective suggestions that foster literacy in school libraries:

**1** Make the school library warm, soft, and inviting. If hard, bare surfaces and shelves exist, cover them with bright, cozy stuffed pillows. Use literacy items, such as colorful book jackets, book-related posters, toys, and stuffed animals, to spark interest and attention. And, don't forget to include "fun writing materials like paper of various sizes, shapes, textures, and colors; an array of pencils, crayons, and markers; and items like tape, staplers, and clips for creating 'books.'"

**2** Make the school library as child-oriented as possible. Include books that have been 'published' by students, by classes, by teachers, by parents, by the librarian, and by the principal. Perhaps a shelf could be labeled "local authors" in the true meaning of those words. Display artwork created by students. Photos of students, teachers, and parents engaged in literacy activities (reading, making grocery lists, readers' theatre) make the purposes for literacy real.

**3** Think about design features and how they can be more child-friendly. For prekindergarten through second grades, popular books could be left open, on shelves, or tables, to snare children into the excitement of books. Often, books placed side by side on the shelves do not give the wonder of what is within.

Librarians, administrators, and teachers all have a role in creating a real literacy environment that will lead to closing the achievement gap in schools. Children need to learn real strategies, read real books, and learn for living in the real world. Scaffolding real literacy needs to be the thrust and sole purpose of schools in the 21st century.

# The Practice

In real literacy-focused schools literacy is celebrated (Cunningham & Allington, 1999). Books of all kinds are at the fingertips of children in classrooms, in the library, and often even in the principal's office (Harwayne, 1999). Word walls displaying important words learned and student work adorn the walls. The hallways and school lobby, too, are filled with information about books, student writing, and demonstrations of how the school values literacy (such as graphs of how many books each class has read). Assessment is a natural process so that the instruction meets the needs of all students. In addition to reading, the areas of writing, listening, and speaking are also integrated throughout the day. (Practitioner books and Web sites that outline how this vision can look are listed under "Practitioner Books" in the "Reading the Minds of Others" section at the end of this chapter.)

Instruction includes explicit teaching of strategies and modeling in whole class and small groups. The instruction is usually precisely delivered in mini lessons. Then, time is given to the students to practice what was taught in many contexts with coaching if necessary. Student choice is an integral part of the practice. Therefore, administrators walking through a building should see short (approximately 10 minutes) lessons and children reading.

Collaboration among all members of the faculty and staff is crucial if a literacy focus is to be initiated and maintained. Research by Allington (2001) states that the amount of reading that children do "in and out of school" directly correlates with student achievement. He even suggests that books should carry a label that says "Regular reading of this product can reduce the risks of acquiring a reading/learning disability" (p. 29). Findings from his research document the importance of having a wide variety of books at different levels of complexity in every classroom; he thus advocates that each classroom should have at least 500 books displayed at all times (p. 55). Therefore, in a literacy-focused school, reading replaces worksheets in every educational activity in the school (library, reading class, content area classes, and the gym) with real books and real-world activities (filling out forms, Internet searches, reading brochures, and so on). The school also needs a well-stocked and well-organized school library with books that will meet the interests and grade levels of all of the children in the school.

One of the major differences between a literacy-focused school and traditional school programs is that the responsibility for this literacy environment is shared. The amount of books in a classroom should not depend any more on the amount of money the teacher personally spends on the classroom library. Every room in the building needs to offer children opportunities to read. Appropriate books need to be bought and circulated throughout the school so children have many choices. When walking into any room, what content area learning is taking place should be apparent by topic books that are displayed. This cooperation occurs when the expertise of all the professionals in the building is maximized.

Teachers need the support of librarians who know how to choose appropriate books and oversee fair and effective circulation of materials throughout the school. This organization requires time for communication of needs and the librarian's expertise. For example, the librarian, if given the time, could assemble grade level collections on content area themes, such as ocean life or the Revolutionary War. Principals can assist in this collaborative effort by adding librarian-teacher planning time as part of the librarian's daily schedule.

In summary, the *practice* in a real literacy-focused school is one where all faculty and staff share the goal of supporting all the children in the school on their paths to literacy. All parts of the school environment demonstrate this literacy focus. Throughout all of the rooms in the school, children are reading. Responsibility for putting the right books in the hand of each child is a shared professional responsibility.

---

Real literacy classrooms should include the following:

- Books, books, and more books;
- A variety of reading materials;
- Cozy, comfortable settings that remind us of home;
- Word walls that work;
- Labels on objects;
- Literacy Centers;
- Display of students' writings;
- Oral language development;
- Interactive read alouds;
- Phonemic awareness;
- Phonics instruction;
- Comprehension strategy instruction;
- Authentic texts; and
- Authentic tasks.

# Professional Development Ideas

Discovering how you feel about writing or that you really have an intense passion for poetry are exciting literacy adventures that can change the way librarians and teachers view themselves as literacy leaders. For example, how and why do librarians select certain materials for their students? How do teachers teach writing, and do they integrate poetry within their content areas? Defining literacy and looking at literacy in their own lives help educators realize how important their roles are to the lives of their students. These discoveries define us as literacy users. They give a strong foundation upon which teachers can build truly insightful lessons that engage our students. These discoveries provide librarians with creative parent-child library newsletters. Step One in beginning a school-wide literacy program is to start with the understandings of librarians, teachers, and principals as they view themselves as literacy learners and users.

One way to begin this literacy self-understanding is to research and develop our own paths to literacy. This journey is called a literacy history or literacy autobiography. In literacy autobiography, librarians, teachers, and principals examine their own literacy. Questions used as professional development might include "When did you first learn to read? Did someone read to you in your home? Can you remember the first book that you owned? What do you read now?"

Begin literacy autobiographies in a school by asking librarians, teachers, and principals some questions, such as those previously suggested. Then, ask them to reflect on these questions, first, by writing their responses, and second, by sharing these responses in small groups. The small groups then report to the entire group interesting findings about their fellow faculty members. Some questions that can be asked include the following:

- What is your favorite book?
- When did you learn to read?
- How did you learn to read and who taught you?
- Do you like to write?
- What do you read now?
- How much time do you spend reading?
- What is the first book you owned?

At the conclusion of this activity, emphasize that what happened was truly a literacy encounter because reading, writing, speaking, and listening occurred.

Another activity for focusing literacy within a school involves asking librarians, teachers, and principals to write their definitions of literacy. In small groups, educators reach consensus on one definition in their group. These definitions are put on chart paper, posted, and shared with the entire group. Then everyone walks around and uses stickers to vote on a first and second choice. The one with the most votes is adopted as the collaborative definition of literacy and can be displayed in the opening hallway of the school, in the library, and in the faculty room.

Biopoems also serve as a powerful tool for self-discovery. As an ice-breaker at a professional development session, have librarians, teachers, and principals compose their biopoems. Sharing the poems creates a sense of community, and we learn a lot about who we are and what we value. Poetic techniques, such as alliteration and metaphor, can be encouraged. These literacy self-reflections provide perfect opportunities to begin the discussion of differing views of literacy.

---

**BIOPOEM DIRECTIONS**

Biopoem Pattern

    Line 1: First name

    Line 2: Four traits that describe character

    Line 3: Relative (e.g., brother, mother) of _____

    Line 4: Lover of _____ (list three things or people)

    Line 5: Who feels _____ (three items)

    Line 6: Who needs _____ (three items)

    Line 7: Who fears _____ (three items)

    Line 8: Who gives _____ (three items)

    Line 9: Who would like to see _____ (three items)

    Line 10: Resident of _____

    Line 11: Last name

** Complete every line in the poem, but do not use the words Line 1, Line 2, and so on. For example, a biopoem on George Washington might begin

George

Honest, brave, patriotic, short

Father of Our Country

Lover of justice, the Bill of Rights, liberty

---

Biopoems can then be used as a literacy instructional strategy within the elementary classroom. One powerful illustration of their use is to have third graders compose a biopoem about a historical person, e.g., George Washington or Rosa Parks. Additionally, children can create their own biopoems throughout the school to be displayed in the hallways.

## Professional Development Through Theory Share

We are what we read.

What does it mean to teach for literacy? Now is the time to grab some of the books on display in the professional development corner of the teachers' lounge or in the school library. Administrators may want to give librarians and teachers professional development time during the school day to browse through them. The field of literacy, especially teaching literacy, undergoes refinements and extensions often.

Two different activities can be done with the books:

■ Each librarian, teacher, and principal chooses a book to browse. They do a quick book walk through the book, looking at pictures, topic areas, and so on. Then, each one shares something interesting that they found in the book.

■ A book pass would also work well. Each librarian, teacher, and principal looks at the books for a couple of minutes. At a signal, that person passes the book to the next person. (This idea is a great activity to do with kids, too.) At the end of the pass, each literacy educator makes a brief statement about the book he or she is holding, Anyone else can give additional information about that book.

## Professional Development Through Experiential Learning

The most successful way we have found to transfer theory to practice is by experiential learning. Visits to literacy-focused schools, libraries, and classrooms where the librarians, teachers, and principals can see the practices in place have proven to be powerful in changing practice. Few librarians and teachers ever get the opportunity to watch other librarians and teachers or to see how other school libraries are organized. A visit and an observation are more productive than words that attempt to explain a situation. The ideal might consist of librarians and teachers spending a day in the host school, observing how other librarians and teachers implement their roles and deliver instruction. If this is not possible, even a visit after school can be productive. In both cases, looking at the environment and student work should be part of the observation.

# The Librarian's Link

Numerous studies have shown a link between increased student achievement and the dynamic utilization of the school librarian (Lance & Loertscher, 2003; Kreschen, 1993; McQuillan, 1998; Russell, 2002). Trained, professional librarians are the experts in the buildings for the following:

■ Buying books,
■ Overseeing the sharing of resources,
■ Using all types of electronic media to support literacy instruction,
■ Creating holistic reading motivation programs that involve the whole school and the community,
■ Collaborating with teachers to create strong literacy-rich units of study, and
■ Becoming professional literacy developers who enable teachers to match books to readers and to provide motivating reading instruction in their classrooms.

The following collaborative possibilities happen in a literacy-focused school if the talents and training of the school library media specialist are utilized:

**1** Teachers and the school librarian collaborate to design content area units. The librarian pulls together books and materials that could be used in the classrooms to supplement the difficult reading of many of the subject area textbooks. When the students from these classes come to the library, the librarian assists them in selecting an area of interest from the topic area and initiates their research on the chosen topic on the Internet. The students write and share this information with classmates to enrich the study of the topic.

**2** At grade level meetings, the librarian shares the importance of having many books in each classroom. Instead of teachers just buying books for their classroom libraries, the school librarian oversees buying a large collection of books for classroom uses and designs a way they can be circulated so that each classroom collection changes periodically. Since a larger amount of books are purchased together, the price per book is usually lower. By having the librarian oversee the purchasing and distribution of the books, all children in every classroom will have opportunities that a quality book collection provides. Children will have access to new books on a periodic basis.

**3** The school library becomes a hub for literacy activity. All grade level book collections are kept there. Librarians select and purchase materials for classroom use, for student borrowing, and for family borrowing. Teachers visit the school library with their students to observe how and why students choose books. Within a dynamic library, librarians model read-alouds, Internet searching, use of different types of media, and booktalks. Modeling of these literacy experiences provides teachers, students, and parents with the necessary tools for them to reap the benefits of the library's myriad resources.

In order for these collaborative literacy experiences to occur, the school librarian must be professionally trained (Hartzell, 2002; Lance & Loertscher, 2003). Some elementary schools are replacing librarians with paraprofessionals who lack the necessary educational background to provide literacy leadership. According to Miller & Shontz (2001), only 61 percent of school media specialists hold a degree in school library media.

Administrators can support the collaborative efforts of librarians by building time into the schedule for the school librarian to oversee the school book collection, to collaborate and plan with teachers, to plan for their own teaching, and to manage the school library. In addition, principals can support librarians and teachers in collaborative literacy endeavors by allocating funds for quality books and materials as a budget priority.

## The Principal's Perspective

Anthony Alvarado (1998), the chancellor for instruction in San Diego (California) City Schools, has become a leader in the effort to develop strong literacy-focused schools. Before working in San Diego, he was the superintendent of District 2 schools in New York City. Under his supervision in both school districts, the increase in student achievement has been dramatic and fast. He suggests one of the keys to these increases is a new kind of collaboration between principals and faculty. The principal has to be involved on a daily basis in "scheduling, arranging, facilitating, and monitoring" (p. 21).

The type of monitoring Alvarado suggests is not an occasional visit to the classrooms, but a daily, active role in watching instruction, coaching teachers, observing librarians, and seeing the growth and needs of children firsthand.

Following the lead of District 2 and San Diego, the Fund for Educational Excellence in Baltimore, Maryland, developed the Achievement First Literacy Initiative in 1999, which has involved more than 40 schools in the Baltimore City Public School System over the last five years. In this initiative, the look and purpose of schools changed, and student achievement did increase. The principal's role in the schools, though, dramatically changed.

Principals attended monthly administrators' meetings to become literacy leaders in their schools. They visited schools in New York City and were mentored by principals from these schools who could share firsthand experiences of how to lead a literacy-focused school. They were required to spend 90 minutes a day in classrooms during the language arts block. In developing their school budgets, 80 percent of their discretionary and Title I funds were to be dedicated to improving literacy. More information about Achievement First can be found on the Fund for Educational Excellence Web site <www.ffee.org>.

Some of the most drastic changes in these schools involve books and the libraries. Most of the schools had out-of-date libraries. Many did not have librarians. Technology was not used, and classroom libraries were nonexistent. Monthly administrators' meetings moved from school to school, included classroom visits, and were usually held in the school library. These libraries are now under the care of trained professionals, and books can be seen throughout the schools. There is no doubt that literacy is their chief concern. The principals take pride in sharing accounts of how literacy is thriving in their schools by showing off their literacy-focused schools. Reporting on collaborations in the schools has become a part of every meeting.

Alvarado suggests that the principal must be wary of "snake-oil" salespeople who try to sell them programs, and learn to "focus on stuff that is important." The principal in a literacy-focused school knows when real literacy practice is happening in the classrooms and in the library.

# The Collaboration

One of the newest movements in whole school change involves the collaboration of all of the major players (faculty, administration, and paraprofessionals) toward focusing all the school's efforts on literacy. In many ways literacy does underline all that happens in schools. Traditionally, both librarians and faculty members have been isolated. The power and energy of differing talents from all members of the school's team, coupled with an acknowledged focus on student literacy, has shown dramatic results in academic achievement in more than 3,000 schools (Lance & Loertscher, 2003; Rolheiser, Fullan, & Edge, 2003).

In this chapter, the discussion of research from many combined fields (reading, library science, educational leadership, and cognitive theory) guided us in developing a vision of schools where all children have opportunities to pursue the use of real literacy (reading, writing, speaking, and listening) in their lives. This vision happens when the learning in each classroom does not depend only on the background and personal resources of the teacher. This vision happens when the expertise of a trained librarian is used to buy appropriate books and literacy materials to meet the interest and reading level needs of all of the children in the school.

This vision happens when the expertise and experience of administrators are combined to support teachers in infusing these real literacy materials into all parts of the instructional day. This vision happens when school budgets focus the majority of resources on literacy in a shared manner throughout the school. Seeking real literacy for all children in a school, which is the only authentic way to raise student achievement, requires a careful consideration of the roles of all the major players and the possibilities that a different understanding of these roles can have in pursuit of this effort.

This chapter described the research that influenced this whole school literacy-focus movement and a vision of how it can look in a school. The possibilities of the roles of the significant players in a school collaborating for higher literacy achievement are also shared. When collaboration transcends isolated practice, real literacy results.

# Reading the Minds of Others

## References

Allington, R.L. (2001). *What really matters for struggling readers: Designing research-based programs.* New York: Longman.

Alvarado, A. (1998). Professional development is the job. *American Educator,* Winter, 18–24.

Bell, L.L. (2003). Strategies that close the gap. *Educational Leadership, 60* (4), 32.

Brandt, D., & Clinton, K. (2002). Limits of local: Expanding perspectives on literacy as social practice. *Journal of Literacy Research, 34* (3), 338.

DeVries, R. & Kohlberg, L. (1987). *Constructivist early education: Overview and comparison with other programs.* Washington, DC: National Association for the Education of Young Children.

Gambrell, L.B. (1996). Creating classroom cultures that foster reading motivation. *Reading Teacher, 50* (1), 14–25.

Gould, J.S. (1996). A constructivist perspective on teaching and learning in the language arts. In C. T. Fosnot (Ed.). *Constructivism: Theory, perspectives, and practice.* (p. 92–102). NY: Teachers College Press.

Guthrie, J.T. (1997). The director's corner. *NRRC News: A Newsletter of the National Reading Research Center* (January).

Hartzell, G. (2002). What's it take? *Teacher Librarian, 30* (1), 81–86.

Kreshen, S. (1993). *The power of reading.* Englewood, CO: Libraries Unlimited.

Lance, K. & Loertscher, D.V. (2003). *Powering achievement 2nd edition: School library programs make a difference.* San Jose, CA: Hi Willow Research & Publishing. Retrieved August 8, 2003, from <http://www.lmcsource.com/tech/power/2nd/power2.htm>.

Lau, D. (2002). *Gotham's grand vision. School Library Journal, 48* (3), 52–52.

McQuillan, J. (1998). *The literacy crisis.* Portsmouth, NH: Heinemann.

Miller, M. & Shontz, M. (2001). New money, old books. *School Library Journal, 47* (10), 50–60.

Ramsey, J. G. (1997.) Literacy. *Vital speeches of the day, 63* (22), 699.

Readence, J.E. & Barone, D.M. (1996). Expectations and directions for Reading Research Quarterly: Broadening the lens. *Reading Research Quarterly, 31* (1), 8–11.

Rolheiser, C., Fullan, M., & Edge, K. (2003). Dynamic Duo. *The Journal of the National Staff Development Council, 24* (2), 38–41.

Russell, S. (2002). Teachers and librarians: Collaborative relationships. *Teacher Librarian, 29* (5), 35–38.

Staton, M. (1998). Reading motivation: The librarian's role in helping teachers develop programs that work. *Library Talk, 11* (4), 181.

Strickland, D.S. Forward. (1999). In L.B. Gambrell, L.M. Morrow, S.B. Neuman, & M. Pressley (Eds.). *Best Practices in Literacy Instruction* (p. xix). NY: Guilford Press.

Teale, W.H. (1999). Libraries promote early literacy learning: Ideas from current research and early childhood programs. *Journal of Youth Services in Libraries, 12* (3), 9–16.

Tompkins, G.E. (2001). *Literacy for the 21st century: A balanced approach. 2nd edition.* Upper Saddle River, NJ: Merrill.

Vygotsky, L.S. (1978). *Mind in Society.* Cambridge: MA: Harvard University Press.

## Practitioner Resources

Cunningham, P. (2002). *Four blocks.* Retrieved August 8, 2003, from <http://www.wfu.edu/~cunningh/fourblocks>.

Cunningham, P.M. & Allington, R.L. (1999). *Classrooms that work: They can all read and write (2nd ed).* New York: Longman.

Dorn, L., French, C., & Jones, T. (1998). *Apprenticeship in literacy: Transitions across reading and writing.* York, ME: Stenhouse.

Fountas, I.C. & Pinnell, G.S. (1996). *Guided reading: Good first teaching for all children.* Portsmouth, NH: Heinemann.

Fountas, I.C. & Pinnell, G.S. (2001). *Guiding readers and writers: Grades 3–6: Teaching comprehension, genre, and content literacy.* Portsmouth, NH: Heinemann.

Harwayne, S. (1999). *Going public: Priorities and practices at the Manhattan New School.* Portsmouth, NH: Heinemann (for Administrators).

Layne, S.L. (2001). *Life's Literacy Lessons.* Newark, DE: The International Reading Association.

McLaughlin, M. & Allen, M.B. (2002). *Guided comprehension: A teaching model for grades 3–8.* Newark, DE: International Reading Association.

Morrow, L.M. (2001). *Literacy development in the early years: Helping children read and write (4th ed.).* Boston: Allyn & Bacon.

Schulman, M.B. & Payne, C.D. (2000). *Guided reading: Making it work.* NY: Scholastic.

# Chapter 2

# Scaffolding: A Key to Real Literacy Instruction

## An Educator's Voice

"Scaffolding is a great way to teach. Too many times we 'stay in the driver's seat' and do not let them take the wheel. Students will not become self-motivated, internalize strategies, or take over in their learning if we don't let them do it on their own. Too many times I have heard teachers say, 'I taught them that strategy but they just won't use it,' and I have said to myself, 'Well, it is because we have not modeled it enough and never let go of their hands.'"

 A First Grade Teacher in Harford County Public Schools, Maryland

## Anticipation Questions

*Before reading this chapter, consider what you already know about the concept of scaffolding.*

 What does it mean to scaffold instruction?
 When you have taught the same children for more than one year, do you find that you are teaching some of the same skills and strategies over and over?
 How much time should be spent teaching one strategy?
 Can you track the steps that you took to learn something new recently?
 Can you define "gradual release of responsibility"?

*In this chapter, learning and teaching in a literacy-focused school will be examined with the concept of independent application of what is being taught in the forefront of all learning.*

## Exploring the Theory

Teaching for literacy demands that instruction focus on individual application. The emphasis is on the learner demonstrating the concept in real literacy events. The teacher skillfully scaffolds the learning so that support is gradually released until the learner independently uses the skill or strategy.

Often, when reflecting on past teaching, we can all remember teaching the same concept or skill over and over, especially when we are librarians or content area teachers who have the opportunity to teach the same children year after year. Why are we constantly teaching the same thing? Researchers suggest that in order to teach for understanding and literacy application that are lasting, we need to gradually release the responsibility for the learning to the learners until they demonstrate proficiency (Cambourne, 1995; Gambrell & Mazzoni, 1999). Key to this concept of gradual release of responsibility is the process of scaffolding instruction instead of just delivering it.

To visualize this concept of scaffolding, think about the scaffolding put up to paint a building. As the building is painted, the scaffolding is gradually taken down until the job is finished and the building is painted. In literacy instruction, at the beginning of teaching a strategy, the teacher gives total support by directly teaching what the strategy is and how to use it. Then, in order for the students to internalize this strategy, the teacher has to gradually release the responsibility for use of the strategy to the learner. The teacher's role then changes from the instructor in front of the students to the coach from behind. Many opportunities are given for the student to practice the strategy in small groups and in pairs. The teacher watches the application of the strategy and pushes in with instructional "talk" only when he sees that additional guidance is needed. The goal for all literacy instruction is for students to be able to demonstrate the strategy in multiple real reading applications. This gradual releasing of the responsibility to the student is the key to dramatically improving test scores since low scores often reflect that the students have not internalized strategies in order to use them in every situation.

Wilkinson & Silliman (2000) imply that classroom language is often the key to literacy learning. They reference numerous research studies that analyze teacher talk in the classroom. These studies suggest that instruction is often dominated by "directive scaffolds" that are "defined by predominance of teacher control mechanisms" and are rooted in educators' beliefs "that the function of instruction is knowledge transmission" (p. 343–344). They conclude that supportive scaffolding following directive scaffolding is crucial to children's literacy development and prevention of reading failure. As a result, they developed the following sequence for instructional conversations that need to take place to release responsibility for literacy to students:

**1** *Explicit modeling* — teacher demonstrates the strategy.

**2** *Direct explanations and re-explanations* — the teacher does not assume they understand the strategy but carefully crafts their conversations to define and apply the concept or strategy over and over until understanding becomes apparent.

**3** *Invitations to participate in the conversation* — the learners share their understandings and support their reasoning.

**4** *Verifying and clarifying student understanding* — the teacher listens for understandings, re-directs misunderstandings, and scaffolds the small steps to better application through questioning and feedback (p. 346–347).

The concept of scaffolding initially evolved from the theories of Vygotsky (1978). He suggested that in order to learn, children need to be taught in their "zone of proximal development," which is the level a little above where the learner can comfortably operate independently. At this level the teacher or adult supports the child's learning with different types of cues and coaching until the learning is demonstrated in independent application.

Cambourne (1995) suggests, "Learning is essentially a process of habit formation" (p. 184) and recommends certain "conditions for learning." The following are the conditions that he identifies:

- *Immersion*, which he defines as "being saturated by, enveloped in, flooded by, steeped in, or constantly bathed in that which is learned" (p. 186).
- *Demonstration*, where the learning is modeled for the learner.
- *Engagement* needs to combine with the immersion and demonstration to create learning. Engagement suggests active participation and desire to learn.
- *Expectations and responsibility* suggest that learners learn when they believe they can learn and make the decision to learn (a step often forgotten by educators). The learner has to feel empowered to grasp the learning.
- *Approximations* are a crucial step to learning. Learners have to feel free to make mistakes in order for the learning to occur.
- *Response* suggests the need for the learner to receive feedback as a consequence of using this learning.
- *Employment* gives the learner many opportunities to use the learning in meaningful ways.
- *Evaluation* is a "continuous thread that runs through any teaching/learning process" (p. 189). Learners have to be led to evaluate their own performance in order to understand how close their approximations are coming to the successful employment of the strategy.
- *Transformation* occurs when the learner takes what is demonstrated and transforms it into some "set of meanings/and or skills that are uniquely theirs" (p. 189).

Teachers use these theories and knowingly teach to release. This process usually includes explicit teaching, modeling, and coaching. Many opportunities are given for the students to demonstrate use of the strategy. The learning environment also provides many supports that enhance the student's responsibility for learning. The teacher comfortably changes her role from the teacher to the coach as needed until she can step back and watch the strategy be applied independently by the learner.

# The Practice

Putting this scaffolding concept into practice requires mapping out the steps it will take to release the responsibility for applying what is being taught by the teacher to the student. Visualize those building scaffolds suggested at the beginning of this chapter. The goal of a literacy teacher is to take the scaffolds away gradually so that the student *automatically* uses the strategy in real reading, as the painter takes away the scaffolds when the work on the building is finished. This automaticity and real reading are the keys. Dittos and worksheets are not *real* reading. The teacher going over the directions is not automaticity. The job is not finished until the students demonstrate independent use of what was taught in materials of their choice.

## The Steps

The following are the basic steps in teaching a strategy or skill using a scaffolding or gradual release of responsibility approach are:

- ■ *Direct Instruction* — The teacher explicitly tells the learner what he is teaching and how to do it.
- ■ *Modeling* — The teacher shows how this strategy is used by demonstrating how she uses it.
- ■ *Coaching* — The teacher chooses opportunities for the learner to try the strategy or skill in small groups, with a partner, and then by themselves. The teacher coaches the small group, intervening when they need more instruction. The teacher watches as the pairs work and again intervenes when instruction is still needed. Finally, the teacher watches as the students choose their own materials and intervenes one-on-one only when needed to guide the student away from a misunderstanding.
- ■ *Independent Application* — The teacher designs opportunities where the students are performing the strategy unaided to determine if they can do it on their own. All directions and application are done entirely by the students on their own. If the students need help, the teacher returns to the coaching model and adds more time until this stage has been reached.

See Figure 2.1 for an example of how to teach the standard "Self-select and independently read fiction, non-fiction and poetry." This example specifically works on the initial component of this standard, which is how to teach a class of young children the difference between fiction, nonfiction materials, and poetry. This strategy is often a beginning one taught by the librarian to young children and is frequently included in Library Media content standards from first to sixth grade. If the concept of gradual release of responsibility is applied to this standard, it needs to be taught only in first grade and then applied in later grades. Notice that this is not a strategy that is taught in one class to the children and they will then automatically apply it. In the gradual release of responsibility model, the strategy is mapped out over a series of classes until the children are doing it independently. Research suggests that if done in this way, children will automatically apply the strategy taught in standardized assessment, in years to come, and in real life.

## Instructional Strategies

When mapping out how to gradually release responsibility for a specific piece of learning, the teacher can choose from a menu of instructional strategies. Instructional strategies are teaching approaches that we use to scaffold instruction. Many teachers use different instructional strategies in their teaching but are not aware of the different levels of scaffolding each one does.

## Teaching the Difference Between Fiction, Nonfiction and Poetry

### Direct Instruction and Modeling

**The librarian/teacher has total control.** The conceptual differences between the three types of text are explained by using a chart that can be displayed in the room. Often the chart is developed with the children. Then using *read-aloud,* the teacher models use of the skill. In this case, the teacher could have three texts (one of each type). She reads a little bit of it and thinks aloud about what type of text it is, referring to the chart for help. She has all of the control, so she does not at this stage ask for the students' help in determining the difference but demonstrates making the decision herself.

### Sharing the Responsibility

**The teacher then gradually releases some of the responsibility** to the children to help to determine what type of reading material each example is and why. To involve all of the children and to assist in understanding which students may not be getting the concept, she could read a selection, let the children share what type of text it is with a person on either side of them, and then poll the whole group on their answer. Again, she leads the students to use the chart to support their decision making.

### Coaching – Giving Over Most of the Responsibility

**Now the teacher steps back** and lets the children try the strategy on their own. Put the children into table groups with a stack of books and a sticky note pad. The children put a sticky note on each book stating whether it is fiction, nonfiction or poetry and supporting their conclusions with information from the chart. The use of the specific reference to the chart is an additional scaffold. The teacher gives help only when needed. If there are students who in the step before that did not understand the concept being taught, she may choose to work with those children in a small group to scaffold their understanding a little more. The other children scaffold each other. At the end of the time, each group may report out by reading the first couple paragraphs of one of their books, sharing what type of material it is, and giving their support from the chart.

### Releasing the Responsibility

**Children are then asked to apply the strategy.** Either by allowing the children to just walk around the library or select from a huge pile of books, each child finds an example of each type of text indicating what type of text it is and how the conclusion was reached.

**Figure 2.1:** A Teaching Example Using Gradual Release of Responsibility

The following are commonly used instructional strategies and a brief description of how the strategy can be chosen for scaffolding purposes:

- **Read Aloud**—Reading aloud to children provides a model for what good readers do. If the teacher adds a "think aloud" component, the modeling becomes more explicit. For example, using the example of understanding the difference between fiction, nonfiction, and poetry given in Figure 2.1, the teacher could read aloud from a poetry book. After reading a stanza of poetry, the teacher would pause and share her thinking. Using a voice that suggests a thinking stance, she may say, "Now, in reading this, I am seeing short lines and rhyming. Both of these are on my chart as characteristics of poetry. I think this is an example of poetry."

- **Charting**—Guide children to make charts together that are displayed in the room. This idea stimulates thinking about the topic, provides opportunities for discussion, and gives the teacher an opportunity to do additional explicit instruction if needed. These charts can act as independent scaffolds for the student to use when she needs help instead of asking the teacher. The charts reinforce a life-long literacy skill, which is the concept of looking in their environment for help. It also gives the child who is a visual learner extra support.

- **Shared Reading**—Using a piece of text either on a chart, overhead transparency, or a paper/book in front of each child, everyone, including the teacher, reads together. The teacher lifts his voice higher if the students need more support. The higher voice is a great way to give help with more difficult words instead of stopping the flow of the reading to sound them out. Next, analysis of the reading for the purpose of the strategy instruction occurs. The teacher is still the leader in this instructional strategy, but he is beginning to let the students have some of the responsibility.

- **Guided Reading**—The teacher chooses a small group of students that need more support. Using the same resource (book, article, and so on), the students read together, either by whisper reading or by reading silently. Whisper reading is a strategy used with young children. All the children whisper the words as they are reading so the teacher can listen to them. Often, the teacher scaffolds this group reading with a deeper discussion of the use of the strategy being taught by chunking the reading into smaller segments. As needed, she may explicitly teach the strategy using a different approach.

- **Small Group Work**—Students in a group work on application of the strategy being taught. In this way, the group members scaffold one another and the teacher can release responsibility. Often, hearing something explained by a peer helps with students' understanding.

- **Literacy Centers**—These areas are set up in the room to give children the opportunity to get needed additional practice of a skill and demonstrate independent application. Chapter 4 goes into more detail on how to use literacy centers.

- **Projects**—These final products are performance assessment at its best. Students are given the opportunity to independently apply the strategy being taught. If the teacher has to give any intervention (e.g., explaining the directions, asking the student to do parts over), then other projects have to be assigned until the students can complete everything independently.

```
┌─────────────────────────────────────────────────────────────────┐
│                                                                   │
│   SCAFFOLDING MAP FOR THE STRATEGY _____        │
│                                                                   │
│   Direct (Explicit) Teaching:                                     │
│                                                                   │
│                                                                   │
│   Modeling (How are you going to show the students how this       │
│   strategy looks in real reading?):                               │
│                                                                   │
│                                                                   │
│                                                                   │
│   Coaching (What is your plan for supporting them from behind?):   │
│                                                                   │
│                                                                   │
│                                                                   │
│   Independent Application (How are you going to tell whether they  │
│   can apply the strategy by themselves?)                          │
│                                                                   │
│                                                                   │
│                                                                   │
│   Note:  Give specific names of materials and instructional       │
│   strategies being used.                                          │
│   Attach examples of independent application activities.           │
│                                                                   │
└─────────────────────────────────────────────────────────────────┘
```

**Figure 2.2:** A Scaffolding Worksheet for Teachers

# Professional Development Ideas

Scaffolding instruction is not a new way of learning. As adults, many of us learn in this way. If you do yoga, how did you learn? Probably someone modeled how to do the moves, you practiced, the teacher watched while giving you tips when you needed them, and when you got the move, you practiced it independently. The key to helping educators understand this concept is by guiding them as they examine how they recently learned something.

Ask librarians and teachers to write down something that they learned to do in the last five years. Ask each to share and form groups with similar activities together. The group can chart the steps that were taken to learn their chosen skills. Have each group share their chart and collaborate to combine all the charts into one cumulative chart.

### Theory Share:

Share the steps of the gradual release of responsibility model, and compare them with the chart that was developed in the section above. Guide the librarians and teachers to understand how experiencing each of the different levels of scaffolding helped them. Keep leading them back to reflect on their own learning.

**The Practice:**

In a follow-up session, share the role each instructional strategy plays. Give specific examples on how to use each strategy. Form groups of librarians and teachers by grade level or by content teaching teams. Using content standards and materials in the school, have them work together to map out a strategy that will be taught by all in the next couple of weeks. Then, provide opportunities during the time of the teaching for the teachers to share successes and problems. At the end of teaching the strategy, the teachers develop one performance assessment to administer to all of the students, score it together, and talk about the results.

# The Librarian's Link

The librarian often is teaching strategies that impact reading in the classroom. Extending the practice of the strategy into the language arts block in the classroom may give important feedback as to whether a strategy is being used independently and can create a closer working relationship between the teachers and the librarian. Also, often the library media content standards closely mirror the language arts content standards. The teacher and librarian working together to scaffold instruction will produce stronger literacy skills and higher test scores.

For example, "the ability to summarize information" often appears in Library Media Content Standards and Language Arts Content Standards. The first step in mastering this standard is for the reader to determine important information in text. How powerful the learning is for the student if both the language arts teacher and librarian are teaching this strategy. With both doing explicit teaching of the strategy, students hear it in different ways, thus appealing to different learning styles. The librarian also has the opportunity to have students apply the strategy using the many resources of the library, e.g. Internet, magazines, poetry, non-fiction, and fiction.

Collaboration that involves scaffolding of students is powerful. Independent practice demonstrations by the students can be shared so that a real understanding of whether they are utilizing the strategy in real situations has a more global meaning. If students are able to apply the strategy, they should be able to do it both in the classroom under the teacher's direction and in the library with the librarian's guidance. If not, the two educators converse about their observations of students to provide more opportunities for the strategies to be learned by all students. In this way both the librarian and the teacher know if the students will independently apply the strategies on assessments.

# The Principal's Perspective

As instructional leader in the building, the principal's understanding of this concept of gradual release of responsibility is essential if student literacy achievement is to rise. Increased student achievement depends on scaffolding instruction to the students' independent levels.

Reading books and articles on this topic can enhance a principal's understanding of scaffolding instruction. Reading the article by Cambourne recommended in "Reading the Minds of Others" gives the principal a better understanding of this concept. The principal's sharing of the article at faculty meetings and talking about it with teachers at pre/post observation meetings will improve instruction within the school.

Creating a framework for instructional planning that is used by all faculty is another step towards changing instruction. The instructional planner explains the steps for gradual release of responsibility, and the educators in the building would be expected to talk about their planning in this way in pre/post conferences and in their daily plan books. A written roadmap of the scaffolding steps can be given to each teacher, with the explicit understanding that such a guide is a mechanism for deeper understanding rather than an evaluative tool. See Figure 2.2 on page 23 for an example.

Principals need to often visit classrooms informally. Achievement First in Baltimore City requires that all administrators spend 90 minutes a day in the classrooms. During this time principals look for independent demonstrations that learning has been internalized. Are the children applying strategies in independent reading? Independent application should be the purpose of all reading instruction. If the principal is not seeing examples of independent application, he needs to share his observations with faculty. For example, if students are working on summary writing, the goal is for children to write a summary without help. If they cannot, the teacher needs to plan more time to scaffold the instruction.

In a literacy-focused school, it is important that the principal suggest ways the library can be used to support literacy efforts. It is in the library that teachers can observe the instructional strategies being used (e.g., librarians often spend more time preparing and using read-alouds than classroom teachers), and watching to see if students independently apply strategies in different types of reading materials (e.g., Internet resources, magazines). Several studies show the significance of the principal's view of the library as a key factor in the success of the collaborative role of the librarian (Bishop & Larimer, 1999; Oberg, 1995). Correlation between the principal's understanding and articulation to teachers of the role of the library in literacy scaffolding and the collaboration that can happen between librarians and teachers and student achievement have been found to be significant (Lance & Loertscher, 2002). Examples of principal scaffolding include the following:

1 Providing staff in-services about the library,
2 Suggesting that teachers who are not effectively using read-aloud or technology resources observe the librarian,
3 Stating expectations of teacher use of the library both at hiring and afterwards, and
4 Serving as a role model by effectively using the library and its resources, especially at faculty and staff meetings.

# The Collaboration

If you walk through a school on any given day, you will often see teachers teaching the same strategies on different grade levels. Instruction in the library, art room, or music room additionally reinforces some of the same strategies and skills. Many times, though, this teaching is not coordinated. Providing time for instructional conversations, collaboration, and observation can make a huge difference in students' independent application of these strategies and skills by coordinating all of this isolated teaching.

The process begins with quality conversations among teachers. Content standards can be the fuel to start these conversations. Standards map out the strategies students need to be literate and build on the previous grade levels. Often, standards from different content areas overlap. Under each strategy, there is a hierarchy of skills to be mastered in order for the learner to be able to effectively use the strategy independently.

Conversations among colleagues about these standards often result in collaboration. For example, a third grade team decides to focus six weeks of instruction in language arts on helping their students towards independent application of the strategy of determining importance. In talking to the primary grade teachers, the third grade teachers realize that their students were taught the skill of main idea, which is crucial to independently applying determining importance. Therefore, rather than teach it again, they do a pre-assessment of the skill and coach only those students who need the extra help. Also, looking at the content standards in social studies, science, library science, and art, they realize that determining importance is crucial to independent work in these subjects as well as language arts. Including the art teacher and the librarian in the planning provides opportunities for additional instruction and support outside the classroom in areas that for some children are more comfortable. Determining importance is crucial to independent work in these subjects as well as language arts. If the art teacher and librarian are also teaching the same strategy, the classroom teacher can observe how the students are applying the strategy in a different setting.

Many opportunities for collaboration happen naturally when the process begins with conversations. This chapter explained the theory of scaffolding and provided much fuel for conversations. The principal's piece in this collaborative effort involves designated time for these conversations.

# Reading the Minds of Others

## References

Bishop, K. & Larimer, N. (1999). Literacy through collaboration. *Teacher Librarian, 27* (1), 15–20.

Cambourne, B. (1995). Towards an educationally relevant theory of literacy learning: Twenty years of inquiry. *The Reading Teacher* 183–190.

Gambrell, L.B. & Mazzoni, S.A. (1999). Principles of best practice: Finding the common ground. In L.B. Gambrell, L.M. Morrow, S.B. Neuman, & M. Pressley (Eds.). *Best Practices in Literacy Instruction.* (p. 11–21). NY: The Guilford Press.

Lance, K.C. & Loertscher, D.V. (2002). *Powering achievement: School library media programs make a difference: The Evidence. 2nd ed.* Spring, TX: LMC Source.

Oberg, D. (1995). *Principal support: What does it mean to teacher-librarians?* (Online). Retrieved Aug. 2000, from <http://www.ualberta.ca/~doberg/prcsup.htm>.

Vygotsky, L.S. *Mind in society.* Cambridge, MA: Harvard University Press, 1978.

Wilkinson, L.C. & Silliman, E.R. (2000). Classroom language and literacy learning. In M.L. Kamil, P.B. Mosenthal, P.D. Pearson, & R. Barr (Eds.). *Handbook of Reading Research: Volume III* . (p. 337–360). Mahwah, NJ: Lawrence Erlbaum, Assoc., Inc.

# Chapter 3

# Literacy Centers: Their Roles in Real Literacy

## An Educator's Voice

"When I used the 'routine' approach and covered the material as our reading series outlined it, my students seemed to never think 'past the book.' Sure, they gave me the answers to questions they were supposed to know, but their learning never seemed to go beyond that."

💬 Intermediate Grade Teacher in Baltimore County Public Schools, Maryland

## Anticipation Questions

*What is your understanding of literacy centers? Consider your answers to the following questions.*

❓ What are literacy centers?
❓ How do they differ from learning centers?
❓ What role do literacy centers have in real literacy?

*This chapter will define literacy centers, show the part they play in the scaffolding process, and give many easy, quick ideas for incorporating them throughout your school.*

## Exploring the Theory

In scaffolding literacy instruction to the independent level, teachers have to ask themselves, "How do I know my students can apply the strategy on their own?" This question is often asked or answered without gathering evidence. David Perkins (1993) suggests that "Teaching is less about what the teacher does than about what the teacher gets the students to do" (p. 31). He further comments, "Understanding performances contrast with what students spend most of their time doing" (p. 29). Literacy centers can play the role of "understanding performances" in a literacy-based classroom if they are designed in a way that shows independent completion of the center as evidence of the student's understanding of what is being taught. The construction of the centers focuses on real reading and writing so that they are "thought demanding ... and take the students beyond what they already know" (Perkins, 1993, p. 29).

Morrow (1997) defines literacy centers as "physical and social contexts ... designed to foster independent participation that is social, collaborative, and cooperative" (p. 3). She describes literacy centers as a collaborative result of research on motivation, integrated language arts, and literacy environments. Morrow explains that literacy centers engage children when:

■ Children are given choices.
■ Children have opportunities for social collaboration within the center activities that are "independent of the teacher."
■ The tasks are challenging, but "able to be accomplished."
■ Children are given some opportunities to share successful tasks with their peers and teachers (p. 5).

Morrow's centers are often content related. Some of her recommendations for literacy centers include listening center, library/independent reading center, writing center, social studies, and science centers, centers for music, and centers for art activities and creative play.

Fountas & Pinnell (1996) define a literacy center as "a physical area set aside for specific learning purposes" (p. 49). They stress the importance of establishing routines for using the centers, introducing them one at a time, and providing all of the necessary materials at the center to complete it. They also suggest that centers need to be organized with the directions and procedures clearly labeled. They recommend using a workboard with icons to identify centers and a way to identify which children are assigned to each center. Some additional centers suggested by Fountas & Pinnell are word work, reading around the room, writing, drama, poetry, buddy reading, reading journals, and games. They also suggest ways to incorporate computers, pocket charts, and overhead projectors. Stone (1996) advocates promoting literacy in all centers, including art, music, math, science, and discovery centers, where students can practice their literacy skills through social interaction, hands-on experiences, and language use.

Neuman (2001) suggests that "a large, varied, and often-refreshed collection of books in the classroom is a vital ingredient in developing early literacy" (p. 12). Neuman lists the following characteristics of a "Literacy-Building Classroom Library":

■ At least seven books per child,
■ Books with a wide range of levels of difficulty,
■ Permanent "core" collection and regularly replenished "revolving" collection,
■ Variety of genres,
■ New books with appealing covers, and
■ An attractive, inviting setting.

Allington (2001) recommends 500 different books in each classroom. He suggests that well-stocked school libraries are crucial to this effort. Libraries should have a very extensive collection of books that can be loaned to classrooms to provide revolving resources for centers and classroom libraries. He emphasizes that in order for this to happen effectively, a library media specialist available on an "as-needed" basis is a crucial component. He further suggests that research "points to the importance of easy access to appropriate texts is at least as important as the number of minutes of planning time allocated, class size, and length of the school day." He also shares that he wonders why the "adequacy of school libraries and classroom book collections are not a key topic in teacher labor agreement negotiations" (p. 60).

Reutzel & Wolfersberger (1996) describe four design concepts in classrooms that affect literacy learning. They believe that children's literacy learning is affected by the following:

**1** The presence or absence of literacy tools,
**2** The arrangement of space and the placement of literacy tools within the arranged space,
**3** Social interaction using literacy tools, and
**4** The authenticity of the context into which literacy tools are placed.

In a similar vein, Patton & Mercer (1996) suggest several basic ideas for transitioning from a teacher-directed classroom to one that is more child-centered. Their ideas include the following:

**1** Start with a few basic centers and add others.
**2** Build upon students' natural enthusiasm by involving them in constructing the centers.
**3** Investigate community resources and thrift shops.
**4** Include books and writing materials.
**5** Incorporate multicultural materials.
**6** Encourage flexibility at the centers by allowing students to move materials to different locations and by not limiting the number of students working together.

Witte-Townsend & Whiting (1999) elaborate on the values of language play that can be incorporated into the centers. They give several suggestions for connecting language development to nursery rhymes, poetry, and songs. For example, *Drummer Hoff* (Emberley & Emberley, 1967) presents opportunities for patterns of contextualized rhyming that support children's development of phonological awareness and their understanding of syntactical relationships among words. Placing this book in the reading center after the class discussion of it strengthens a child's growing sense of word patterns and rhymes. Students could then compose their own variations of the stories, such as "Farmer Blorn, Planted the Corn" (with rhyming words listed in the literacy center).

McLaughlin & Allen (2002) extend the literacy center concept for use in grades 3–8 in their model of "Guided Comprehension." They stress that if designed effectively, these centers can "promote the integration of reading, writing, and discussion" (p. 41). They emphasize that the "content of the center is more important than its physical appearance" (p. 41). These researchers stress the importance of centers having an accountability mechanism. Suggestions for accountability include a reflection journal or a finished product. All of their centers focus on ways students can demonstrate application of reading strategies and include the following additional ideas for developing literacy centers:

- Book making center,
- Vocabulary center that includes activities such as word sorts, acrostics, and word riddles,
- Research center where students research information relevant to content they are studying,
- Genre center that changes according to what is being studied,
- Mystery center where the students either read or write mysteries, and
- Project centers that focus on extending what the children are learning to "multiple modes of response" (p. 51).

Ford and Opitz (2002) suggest that for centers to be effective, children should be working independently. For this to happen, the teacher needs to observe the children engaged in independent activities, evaluate their progress without teacher intervention, and plan further instruction to make them successful. Mini lessons are used to teach children procedures. Centers should be simple to construct and change. State and local curriculum can be embedded in center activities.

Gunning (2003) also suggests that centers should be connected to the curriculum and have objectives that show a direct connection to standards being studied. He specifies that centers include a title, activities, directions, materials, and assessment. The assessment should be some type of accountability instrument to track the progress of the students at the center. Some suggestions that he offers are using a form at the reading center to record pages read or a piece of writing that is produced as a result of doing the center activity.

Cambourne (2001) collected data to determine what successful teaching/ learning activities looked like. The teachers in his study shared the need for students to be deeply engaged for learning to take place. Following are his suggestions for teaching/learning to be successful:

- The students had to be deeply engaged.
- The students had to apply what was "learned in one context to a different context" (p. 126).
- The activities should promote "collaboration, independence, and interdependence in the learners" so teachers can successfully work with small groups (p. 126).

The teachers always linked explicit teaching with their expectations of the end products, and explicitly teach and demonstrate the strategies multiple times before assigning independent practice at literacy centers.

Mackey, Pitcher & Wilson (2002) researched the role principals play in the literacy achievement of second grade students and found that literacy centers were a crucial component of change in the highest achieving school. In the year of the study, the principal of the highest-achieving school hired an outside consultant to train his teachers on the development and use of literacy centers. He then provided each teacher with materials for centers (bins, center signs, folders, and so on) and purchased a classroom library for each room. He also personally monitored each room during the daily 90-minute language arts block to help teachers with the use of the centers. His approach to implementing literacy centers contributed to an approximately 30-point gain in reading achievement scores.

# The Practice

---

## What Do Literacy Centers Look Like?

- ■ A sign identifies the center.
- ■ Directions that students can follow independently are easily seen.
- ■ All supplies necessary to complete the center activities are placed at the center in an organized way.
- ■ Books are a part of each center and displayed in a way that grabs the students' interest.
- ■ Center materials include many reading levels to meet the needs of all of the students in the class.
- ■ A very clear purpose or objective connected to standards is posted.
- ■ A product or accountability measure showing that the activity was completed is provided.
- ■ A defined space to complete the activity is clearly presented to the students.
- ■ Student choice should be included to enhance engagement. The students could choose the book, the accountability sheet, or whether to work alone or with a partner.

---

Literacy centers can be very simple to make:

- ■ *Center titles* — can be made on a word processor with clip art. The center titles and icons are introduced when you first use the center and remain as a natural part of the room. The same titles and icons can be used throughout the school to facilitate children participating in centers in different rooms (library, art, and so on).
- ■ *Books and materials* — poetry books, information books, dictionaries, and so on are left at the center. They can be changed on a rotating basis if materials are available in the school library for this purpose.
- ■ *Directions* — can often be used at more than one center. For example, you may be teaching students to write a summary of what they read. In a mini lesson, writing a summary is introduced using a visual. Put copies of that visual at each center. The students write summaries in different genres until they internalize the concept.
- ■ *Accountability activities* — can also be the same at different centers. To return to the previous example, the directions may be the same at each center. They can

be as simple as following the visual on writing a summary at each center. The directions include steps to choose a reading material from the center (picture book, chapter, poem, information book, or article), read, and write a summary. What makes the center different is the genre of the reading materials.

Centers are not about lots of different activities with fancy, time-consuming, cluttered displays. Centers are about giving students multiple opportunities to practice strategies and skills in different types of reading materials on an independent reading level.

---

### Literacy Centers Support What You Are Teaching

Some centers that are appropriate for any classroom include the following:

■ Poetry,
■ Reading for Information (nonfiction materials),
■ Writing,
■ Library or Reading,
■ Word Work,
■ Listening,
■ Research, and
■ Read Around the Room (only a clipboard and paper are needed to do this center — students use the room for word study).

---

Centers can also be geared to practicing strategies in content areas or specific genres:

■ Art Center,
■ Science Center,
■ Social Studies Center,
■ Mystery Center,
■ Project Center,
■ Research Center, and
■ Music Center.

**IMPORTANT TIP:** The school librarian can be a powerful source for content area center materials. If a class is studying about animals, ask the librarian for help. In addition to animal books from the library displayed throughout centers in the room, other reading materials could be Ranger Rick Magazines, information, schedules from local zoos, or brochures from wildlife groups. With the help of a professional school librarian, teachers can move beyond the textbook to discover a variety of resources readily available within the library and the school.

## A Workboard Is the Key to Successful Centers

Workboards manage the process so that children work independently, know where they are expected to be without wasting classroom time, and know how to go from one activity to another.

Workboards:

■ Use icons that represent each center.

■ List names of children who go to each center. This list can be a laminated chart where names can be written in, magnets on a board where names are on the magnets and can be put under magnets of the icons, or a chart stand where the names are indicated by clothespins. Student names could also be listed on an overhead where the teacher writes in the names of the children assigned to each area. Change names daily or weekly to meet the design of either daily or weekly center activities.

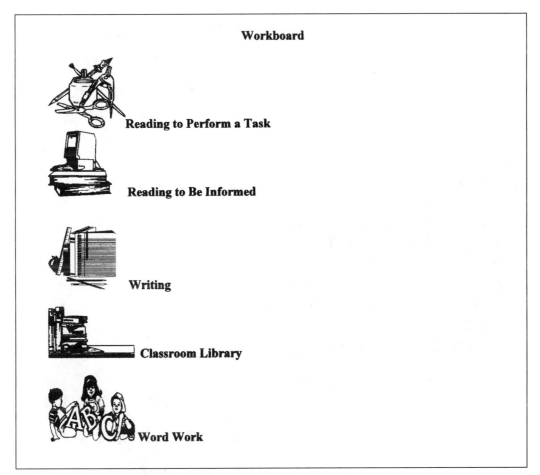

**Workboard**

Reading to Perform a Task

Reading to Be Informed

Writing

Classroom Library

Word Work

**Figure 3.1:** An Example of a Literary Center Workboard

*This workboard can be reproduced on a transparency to use on an overhead projector or blown up on a poster maker and laminated. Names of students working in a center are just written in each day by the teacher. If you want the students to go to more than one center, put the numbers 1 and 2 after their names. The graphics can also be blown up and put on the literacy center signs.*

## Some Examples of Easy Center Activities

1. Choose a book (poem or article could be substituted to use at other centers) from the center.
2. After reading it, state the main idea on the paper provided.
3. Determine four important statements from the article that support the main idea.

In a book of your choice, find as many words as you can with the "at, ap, or an" chunks in them.

Choose a book (poem, article). After reading it, retell what you read on the paper provided. If you need help, use the chart on the wall that lists the steps in retelling. Retelling could also be an interactive activity by having the students find a partner with whom to retell the story.

Read around the room to find two-syllable words. Highlight the chunks in the syllables that you know.

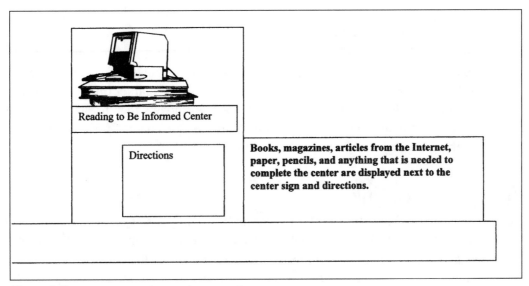

**Figure 3.2:** The Layout for a Literacy Center

# Professional Development Ideas

Often educators confuse literacy centers with the old-style learning centers. To keep old file-folder games from suddenly reappearing in classrooms, begin by accessing what is known. Using the Anticipation Questions in the beginning of this chapter will help to engage the audience in checking their understanding of literacy centers and their purposes. In small groups, the teachers could generate answers to the questions and chart them. If you want the teachers to examine their own understandings, have them write the answers to the questions and revisit them at the end of the professional development session.

## Theory Share:

It is crucial to give teachers a chance to personally read the research before initiating the practice. The Exploring the Theory section of this chapter could be used in a staff development session by doing a read-around. Have all of the teachers read the first and the last paragraph since these readings give a cognitive foundation to the theory. Assign a teacher to read and summarize each of the other paragraphs, giving a quick overview of the research base. The professional books cited in Reading the Minds of Others could be displayed and available for the teachers to borrow for browsing at home.

## The Practice:

A successful way to share the practice of literacy centers is in a "make it and take it" setting. Set up simple, easy-to-assemble centers as models. Provide a packet of some easily adaptable accountability sheets (e.g., simple bookmarks that could be filled in, sentence starters). Next, set up centers with materials to make workboards, a poetry center, a word work center, and so on. Provide bins to put the materials in and a laminator to finish the materials. "Make it and take it" sessions provide wonderful professional development ideas that teachers can easily implement. The literacy environment of an entire school can be transformed in one day with this kind of activity.

## An Inexpensive Tip:

For a word work center, bags of letters or chunks of most used patterns (at, op, in, and so on) can be made using dried lima beans, permanent fine-tipped markers, and self-sealing plastic bags. Letters are written with the marker on the lima beans. The chunks are also written on the lima beans. The students then try to make words by combining letters and chunks. This idea also can be adapted for older students by making bags of root words, suffixes, and prefixes.

# The Librarian's Link

As suggested by Allington (2001) at the beginning of this chapter, the library media specialist can be crucial in making literacy centers and classroom libraries work in schools. The library can become the school model for the construction and use of literacy centers. The librarian is the school specialist on books and, therefore, is the natural leader in this effort.

With suggestions of seven books per child (Neuman, 2001, p. 12) and 500 per classroom (Allington, 2001, p. 55), the question becomes: "How do we make this happen?" The librarian who orders and houses large collections of books that are the integral ingredient in centers is the answer. Books could be organized in bins according to reading levels and then circulated from classroom to classroom. This task provides a wonderful opportunity for librarian-teacher collaboration, as insights and expertise of both are necessary for accurate assessment of leveling texts. A common guide used in elementary schools to level texts is Fountas & Pinnell's book *Matching Books to Readers: Using Leveled Books in Guided Reading, K–3* (2001). This guide includes suggestions on collaboration and lists the reading levels of more than 7,500 books for primary readers. A monthly rotation date would be designated to give each classroom ample time for using each bin. The librarian can also develop genre bins of poetry centers or expository texts for interdisciplinary centers that link science/social studies with literacy for teachers to borrow.

One of the reasons that many teachers do not implement literacy centers is that they simply do not have the money to buy the books or knowledge of what books are appropriate. The librarian could provide both the source and the expertise. Allington (2001, p. 56) suggests that putting money into school libraries to provide a large number of books so they can be lent to teachers is one of the most effective uses of school money (and much more cost-effective than expensive reading series).

At the William Baer School in Baltimore City, Maryland, the library became a hub of literacy and a model for the use of literacy centers in the school. With the support and vision of the principal, Dr. Shari Johnson, and the assistant principal, Rita Jeffers, the librarian, Ronalda Jordan, set up literacy centers for craft activities, reading for information, word study, and science investigations. The William Bear School is a primary school for children with disabilities. In addition to the usual literacy center materials, these centers included adaptive technology to make the engagement in literacy accessible to all. Seeing the enthusiastic engagement of the children in the library was very infectious, and teachers soon developed similar centers in their classrooms.

When Rita Jeffers became principal of Thomas G. Hayes School in Baltimore, she again used the library as a model for a new literacy initiative that she was implementing in the school. Literacy centers (Reading to Be Informed, Reading for Information, Reading to Perform a Task, and a Word Work Center) transformed the library into a hub of literacy engagement. The centers were designed so that the tasks could easily be changed to parallel what was being studied in language arts classes.

Maria Stover, the librarian, met with teachers to coordinate the activities in the library with the content being taught in the classrooms. Instead of making library time a free period for teachers, the teachers came to the library with their students and observed as Maria managed the centers. Since they were collaborating on what was being taught, the teachers could observe how their students were independently applying the strategies that had been taught in another setting. Many of the teachers in this school were new to education, and this modeling became crucial to their implementation of centers.

Literacy centers are a natural extension of what librarians do best. Whether it is managing a large scale, school-wide circulation of books to be used in centers or setting up the school library as a model, librarians make natural leaders in this effort. Librarians feel passionate about placing quality books in the hands of children and thus increasing the amount of independent reading time as a by-product of literacy centers.

# The Principal's Perspective

After 12 years of being a principal, James Smith decided it was time that he "pushed up his sleeves" and "got involved" in his school's literacy program. His school, Arlington Elementary in Baltimore City, was a Title I school with low reading performance. Literacy centers and classroom libraries were one of his first focuses.

Purchasing books and materials for the centers was step one. The librarian ordered books that could be circulated into classroom libraries and materials necessary for the design and use of literacy centers. Information books and poetry, letter tiles and manipulatives, clipboards, and bins were bought and circulated among the teachers in the school.

A literacy consultant conducted staff development sessions with his teachers. Teachers learned about the research that underpinned the development of centers, made workboards and centers, and received books and materials to incorporate in those centers. The staff development session was held in the school library with the librarian displaying books that could be borrowed and used in the centers.

Arlington's librarian also demonstrated many ways to use computers to support this literacy effort. She showed ways to incorporate MS Word into centers in the library and found Internet resources to support content area topics. She helped teachers to use the computers to create center signs and directions.

The literacy environment of this school changed almost overnight. The library became a resource for the development of future centers. Mr. Smith followed up this activity by personally monitoring the implementation of centers. In observing centers being used in classrooms, he looked for the following:

- Authentic activities for the students,
- Reading and writing as a crucial part of center work,
- A management system to assign the students to the centers, and
- Ways he could support teachers in purchasing materials and continuing their professional development.

The literacy achievement in this school increased considerably on both state and district measures and sustained that increase the following year. Teachers were excited about increased student engagement in literacy and their professional growth. Mr. Smith's efforts demonstrate the crucial role a principal plays in implementing literacy centers in a school. This role includes the following:

- Reading the research and personally leading literacy efforts,
- Providing books and materials necessary for implementation, and
- Monitoring efforts and supporting teachers as they implement literacy centers in their classrooms.

# The Collaboration

Literacy centers are a great vehicle for beginning literacy collaboration throughout a school. At professional development meetings, introduce centers by sharing the theory so everyone understands that literacy centers are easy to develop, very important for evaluating independent application of what is learned, and require little management if introduced properly and designed to meet the needs of all learners. The principal provides materials to make centers happen and supports coordination to help them thrive. In this collaborative model, a school environment can be transformed to one that is literacy-centered in a short amount of time.

Ideas that are shared across all literacy stakeholders can make this process more dynamic. For example, teachers can agree to use the same icons for the centers and make workboards together. Children then move easily from room to room, understanding the procedures in the centers. Opportunities to visit one another's classrooms can give teachers new ideas for sharing materials. With the librarian in charge of buying quality materials for the centers and overseeing their distribution, all children in the school will have an equal opportunity for the engagement these centers can provide. Teachers can use their grade level meeting time to discuss and make centers.

Suggestions and procedures to create collaborative efforts for developing literacy centers were discussed in this chapter. An initial step in developing literacy centers is to help teachers understand the theories the development of centers is based upon. Literacy centers are about simplicity and real literacy application.

# Reading the Minds of Others

## References

Allington, R.L. (2001). *What really matters for struggling readers: Designing Research-Based Programs*. NY: Addison-Wesley Educational Publishers. **K–12 Focus**

Cambourne, B. (2001). What do I do with the rest of the class? The nature of teaching-learning activities. *Language Arts, 79*, 124–135. Symbolic plan and literacy learning: classroom materials and teachers' roles. *Reading Improvement, 35* (4), 172–177. **K–8 Focus**

Emberley, B. & Emberley, E. (1976). *Drummer Hoff*. New York, NY: Simon & Schuster.

Ford, M.P. & Opitz, M.F. (2002). Using centers to engage children during guided-reading time: Intensifying learning experiences away from the teacher. *Reading Teacher, 55*, (8), 710–717. **K–5 Focus**

Fountas, I.C. & Pinnell, G.S. (1996). *Guided reading: Good first teaching for all children*. Portsmouth, NH: Heinemann. (Chapters 4 & 5). **K–2 Focus**

Fountas, I.C. & Pinnell, G.S. (2001). *Matching books to readers: Using leveled books in guided reading K–3*. Portsmouth, NH: Heinemann.

Gunning, T.G. (2003). *Creating literacy instruction for all children*. NY: Allyn and Bacon. (Chapter 10). **K–5 Focus**

Mackey, B., Pitcher, S.M., & Wilson, G.P. (2002). *The influence of the principal in four literacy programs*. Presentation given at the International Reading Association Annual Conference, San Francisco, CA.

McLaughlin, M. and Allen, M.B. (2002). *Guided comprehension: A teaching model for grades 3–8*. Newark, DE: International Reading Association. (Chapter 3). **3–8 Focus**

Morrow, L.M. (1990). Preparing the classroom environment to promote literacy during play. *Early Childhood Research Quarterly, 5*, 537–554. **PreK–3 Focus**

Morrow, L.M. (1997). *The literacy center: Contexts for reading and writing*. York, MA: Stenhouse Publishers. **PreK–3 Focus**

Neuman, S.B. (2001). The importance of classroom library. *Early Childhood Today, 15* (5), 12–14.

Patton, M.M. & Mercer, J. (1996). "Hey! Where's the toys?": Play and literacy in 1st grade. *Childhood Education, 73*, 10–16. **Grade 1 Focus**

Perkins, D. (1993). Teaching for Understanding. *American Educator: The Professional Journal of the American Federation of Teachers, 17* (3), 8, 28–35. **K–12 Focus**

Reutzel, R. & Wolfersberger, M. (1996). An environmental impact statement: Designing supportive literacy classrooms for young children. *Reading Horizons, 36*, 266–282. **PreK–3 Focus**

Stone, S. (1996). Promoting literacy through centers. *Childhood Education, 72,* 240–241. **K–8 Focus**

Witte-Townsend, D. & Whiting, A. (1999). Lessons in sweet words: Language play in the elementary school classroom. *The New England Reading Association Journal, 35,* (1), 7–15. **PreK Focus**

# Chapter 4

# Family Literacy: Creating Partnerships for Real Literacy

## An Educator's Voice

" 'Every time I think of walking in the school door, I get sick to my stomach. The idea of going back there for any reason terrifies me'. This statement reflects a fear held by one of the hardest-to-reach segments of the adult population—under-educated parents who believe they can never be part of 'the system.' It is this segment that family-literacy programs try to reach."

Sharon Darling (1994), Director, The National Center for Family Literacy

## Anticipation Questions

*Before reading this chapter, examine your own understandings of family literacy from both a school and a personal perspective.*

- ❓ How is family literacy different from parent involvement?
- ❓ What do you consider "good" participation from parents? Look at the percentage of parents who participate in your school programs. Is it 90%, 10%, or somewhere in between?
- ❓ How was literacy valued in your home when you were growing up? Were you read to? Were there books in your home? Did you go to the library regularly?

*As you read this chapter, your personal experiences and school experiences with family literacy will play a role in how you respond to the research and to the practice.*

## Exploring the Theory

Susan Neuman (1997) says:

> Family literacy is not about changing people; it is about offering choices and opportunities for families. Parents come to family literacy programs with rich histories and experiences that should be honored and used in program development. Family literacy learning is a matter of "small wins." Family literacy is about

providing context, resources, and opportunities for families to demonstrate what they already know and can already do. Family literacy programs MUST respond to parents' needs and interests. Family literacy is about power. ■ (p. 1)

Do schools consider the needs, choices, and opportunities of parents in decisions on parent involvement programs? Auerbach (1995) suggests that parent involvement is defined often by what the school wants the parents to do and not what the parents need. When asked about parent involvement, schools often list activities such as fund raising, parent conferences, and workshops for parents on what parents should do.

Morrow (1995) advises that "'family literacy' does not have a clear definition" (p. 7). Researchers stress the importance of understanding the strengths of families by not developing programs that are intrusive of their cultures or emphasize their deficits (Morrow, 1995; Auerbach, 1995; Neuman, 1997; Padak & Rasinski, 1994). Family literacy does not have a "clear definition" because programs need to be customized to serve the families of differing school communities.

Taylor (1983) first used the term "family literacy" when she studied six highly literate families over three years to capture how literacy was transmitted naturally to the children by the parents. Most of the parents were college graduates, and over half had doctoral degrees. Taylor lived in the community and socialized with the families. She revealed literacy interactions such as reading, writing, and discussions were an integral part of most family activities.

In another study, Taylor, with Dorsey-Gaines (1988), studied four families for six years living in poor areas of New York City by examining both their literacy interactions and their interactions with schools. The researchers shared many examples of how parents tried naturally to give literacy to their children, but lack of materials, serious family illnesses, housing problems, and mothers' low self-esteem complicated literacy interactions. The researchers discovered that families often use junk mail for reading and writing materials. When a reader was sent home with one of the children, the family used this book for many literacy activities, such as read-alouds, discussions, and writing.

Morrow (1983) conducted a study examining differences between children entering first grade with a high interest in reading and those with a low interest. Through home visits and surveys, she tried to capture the literacy interactions in these homes. She found:

■ 95% of the mothers of the high interest readers read novels in comparison to 10.5% of the mothers of the low interest readers.
■ 78.6% of the mothers and 60.7% of the fathers of the high interest readers listed reading as a leisure activity in comparison to mothers (28.1%) and fathers (15.8%) of the low interest readers.
■ Books were in 100% of the bedrooms of children in the high interest groups and only in 16.9% of the low interest group's bedrooms.
■ Many of the parents of the low interest group did not see the relationship of reading activities in the home to reading instruction in school (p. 225).

Heath (1983) also conducted research on literacy interactions in homes. Between the years of 1969 and 1977, she studied two very different communities: white families in Roadville who were moving toward suburban living, which she calls "mainstream," and black families of Tracton who traditionally were farmers but found themselves scattered and living apart from their families in cities. This move was necessary for the Tracton families to receive government assistance. The culture of the Roadville families was very similar to the culture in school, but the Tracton families' home culture was very different from the school culture. The Tracton parents viewed their responsibility for their children to revolve more on punishment than discourse. They looked to the school for all of their children's literacy support.

Bus, Ijzendoorn, & Pellegrini (1995) focused on the literacy influence of parent/preschooler joint reading as it related to language growth, emergent literacy, and reading achievement. From their analysis of 29 studies, they discovered that parents and children reading together was a powerful influence that impacted how children learn to read.

Edwards (1999) challenged us to listen to parent stories because she, too, had seen a lack of understanding and connection between what happens in schools and what happens in homes. She suggested, "Many parents remain completely isolated from the schools, because they have been alienated from schools in the past, or perceive themselves as not having enough time and opportunity" (p. xv). She proposed ways to question parents so educators can better understand how the parents perceive their roles in developing their children's literacy. She suggests that educators should ask parents about their school experiences and how schools can help to support literacy in their homes.

DeBruin-Perecki & Paris (1997) attempted to identify all of the family literacy programs in the state of Michigan and found 50 programs. They chose two programs that were considered effective in their communities. From their extensive analysis of these two effective family literacy programs, four "critical and comprehensive factors that need to be considered" in designing effective Family Literacy programs emerged:

■ *Participation* — Important factors that influence participation, such as transportation, child care, fear of school, low self-esteem of parents, and respect of cultural and family differences, need to be addressed.

■ *Curriculum* — Activities that are "meaningful and useful in the participants' lives" should be presented. Especially important were activities that were developmentally appropriate for both adults and children, allowing and encouraging time on intergenerational activities (p. 9). Successful activities built bridges between home and school, parents and teachers.

■ *Staff and administration* — A collaborative staff with differing community experiences and knowledge was a necessity for effective family literacy programs (p. 9). Additionally, staff training addressing needs, communication with program participants, and an understanding of the community culture was crucial.

■ *Fund raising* — Funds for an effective program came from stable sources to give the staffs and the participants a sense of confidence of the continuity of the program over time.

Opening its doors in 1989, The National Center for Family Literacy has become a national leader of programs that serve the whole family. NCFL programs include adult education, early childhood education, and PACT (Parents and Child Together) Time. In this model, the parent and child education programs are housed together so that parents come into the early childhood classroom to practice interactive reading with their children. The Kenan Project, which started in Kentucky in the late 1980s, was the first program to use this model. "Intensive training for provider staff" contributed to the success of this program (Brizius & Foster, 1993). Other NCFL model programs include Toyota Families for Learning Project and Even Start, a federally funded initiative (NGA Center for Best Practices, 2002).

Neuman & Caperelli (1998) reviewed 52 Barbara Bush Foundation for Family Literacy grants. The Foundation has provided grants in 34 states to support family programming (p. 244). They suggest that the following principles might be "useful for conceptualizing new efforts to support families in a myriad of ways" (p. 250):

- Family literacy is not something that can be "done" to people.
- Family literacy is not about changing people but about offering choices and opportunities to families.
- Parents come with rich histories and experiences that should be honored and used in program development.
- Family literacy programs have both direct and indirect benefits.
- Family literacy learning is a matter of "small wins" (p. 250–251).

# The Practice

The lobby of Bay Brook Elementary School in Baltimore City welcomes parents and families to come in and read. The lobby has comfortable chairs, a sofa, baskets of books, and magazines that appeal to all members of the family. Welcome signs shine throughout the lobby. The principal, Lydia Foster, and her staff chose to redesign the lobby to make the focus of the school very apparent to all entering. At the time she took over the leadership, the school was the lowest-achieving school on Maryland's State Performance Tests. After only one year, the reading scores in the school tripled. This lobby gave a very clear message to parents about what was happening throughout the school.

A welcoming atmosphere and activities for the whole family provide models of literacy that can be transferred to homes. Family literacy activities should incorporate a feeling of welcome and enjoyment of literacy. Activities range from whole school activities, small group activities, class activities, and activities to send home. A focus on family literacy also presents an excellent opportunity for literacy collaboration among administrators, librarians, and teachers.

As suggested by research on effective family literacy programs, the needs and interests of the parents as well as the children provide the focus for the planning and implementing of all activities. Transportation, babysitting, time of day, and food are all crucial for programs offered at schools. Educators can take time, perhaps at the beginning or end of the school day, to ask parents what they need. Surveys often are not the best way to gather parent information because only the most literate parents complete and return surveys. Establishing a parent advisory group to give advice and input will aid in determining which factors in the community need to be addressed for successful programs.

Sharing the educational purposes of family literacy activities with parents is also an important component of a successful family literacy program. An essential step in advertising and sharing these activities is to clearly articulate to parents why the activities are important and how they will benefit from participating in them. Understanding the educational purposes of the activities also allows the literacy stakeholders in a school to have a shared vision of the objectives of the activities when they invite families to participate.

## Group Activities

### Parent Book Club

Using "read aloud" books, kindergarten parents learn strategies such as the following:

- Predicting (What do you think will come next?),
- Chiming (In a book with repetitious phrases, the child learns to repeat those phrases.),
- Rhyming (Using books with rhyming words, such as poetry or nursery rhymes, the child tries to predict the word from the previous rhyming pattern.),
- Making Connections (The child is encouraged to connect what is read to their lives.), and
- Clarifying and Labeling (What is this?).

The facilitator of the Parent Book Club session explicitly teaches the strategy and then models a "read-aloud" of the selected book. Parents practice reading the book with partners, and later visit the kindergarten classroom to read it to their child. The family keeps the book.

The Parent Book Club can provide a great opportunity for collaboration between the school librarian and the kindergarten teachers. The librarian conducts the Parent Book Club by demonstrating the "read-alouds," suggesting additional books for practicing the strategy, and introducing the literacy-rich environment of the library to the newest parents in the school community. A section of the library can feature additional books that aid in practicing these skills. Parents or children are encouraged to check out these books. The parents, welcomed by the kindergarten teachers, read to the children in the classrooms. This collaboration demonstrates to the parents that both teachers and the librarian are working together for their children's literacy and value the parents' participation in their children's literacy.

**Books:**
*Predicting*—*Cat and Dog Make the Best, Biggest, Most Wonderful Cheese Sandwich* by Kimberlee Graves (1997, Creative Teaching Press, Inc.)
*Chiming and Rhyming*—*Over in the Meadow* based on original by O. A. Wadsworth and illustrated by D. A. Carter (1992, Scholastic) and *Yucka, Drucka, Droni* by V. Radunsky (1998, Scholastic)
*Making Connections*—*David Goes to School* by David Shannon (1999, Scholastic) and *Sophie* by Mem Fox (1997, Voyager Books)

*Clarifying and Labeling*—*Dogs Don't Wear Sneakers* by Laura Numeroff
(1993, First Aladdin Paperbacks)

*Adapted from Families Reading Together Program (Philadelphia, PA)*
*Lesson plans that focus on teaching these strategies are available online at*
*<www.towson.edu/~spitcher>.*

**Comprehension Book Club**
This club is an adaptation of the Parent Book Club. The Comprehension Book Club includes the whole family. Parents are taught reading comprehension strategies. The facilitator explicitly teaches the strategy and models it by reading aloud the books and thinking aloud about how they are using the strategy. Next, parents practice the strategy by reading and thinking aloud to each other. Then they read the book to their children. Books are chosen for their special appeal to the parents as well as the children. As parents are learning about the strategy, children are participating either in a craft activity or a reading activity. Again, the librarian would be a great facilitator for this project, providing the parents with a link to other books to continue practicing the strategies.

**The Strategies:**

■ Making Connections—connecting what is read to self, the world, or other texts,
■ Visualizing—making pictures in your mind as you are reading,
■ Inferring—what are the underlying meanings in the story? and
■ Retelling—being able to retell the story.

**Books:**
***Making Connections***—*Amazing Grace* by M. Hoffman (1991, Scholastic)
***Visualizing***—*Verdi* by J. Cannon (1997, Harcourt, Brace & Co.)
***Inferring***—*My Ol' Man* by P. Polacco (1997, Scholastic) and *A Snow Story* by M. J. Leavitt (1995, Simon & Schuster)
***Retelling***—*The Patchwork Quilt* by Valerie Flournoy (1985, Scholastic) and *Harvey Potter's Balloon Farm* by J. Nolen (1994, Scholastic)

*Developed by Parents and Reading Committee, State of Maryland Council of the International Reading Association*
*Lesson plans on teaching each strategy are available online at*
*<www.towson.edu/~spitcher>.*

**Computer Nights**
Computers are a great hook. Computer Nights can be done on a weekly basis or as a one-night activity. The activities can include games that require reading or Internet searches. Often, Computer Nights provide a chance for students to shine and teach some tricks to parents. Especially in areas where families do not own computers, activities that require computer access give families knowledge of computer and Internet tools.

The school librarian or media specialist, usually the most knowledgeable about appropriate Internet sites and available software in schools, would be a natural leader in planning and facilitating computer events. Teacher participation, too, is crucial. Parents often come to events to see and be seen by the teachers. In addition, teachers will learn new Internet sites and software activities, thus providing an atmosphere where all are learning together. Parents who work in fields of technology can also be invited to lead sessions and share their expertise. Computers and technology often provide a perfect intergenerational literacy opportunity because adults and children learn together while sharing common interests and experiences.

**Fun with Reading Night**
The key to making Fun with Reading Night successful is designing activities that all members of the family will enjoy. Participation of the principal, teachers, and the librarian makes the event more appealing to parents and children. Transportation and dinner for the families combine to make Fun with Reading Night a special time. Literacy activities that can be enjoyed by all include the following:

- *Craft Activities* — the art teacher would be a great leader in this activity.
- *Cut Up Comics* — families work together to put cut-up comics from the newspaper in order.
- *Card Games with Directions* — games such as Concentration, Hang Man, Jeopardy, and Trivial Pursuit can be played in groups. Always give out written directions that can be taken home, and explain how they can be adapted to playing at home.
- *A Scavenger Hunt for Information in the Library* — the school librarian leads this activity. Families discover parts of the library that may be new to them by going on a scavenger hunt to find selected information or books. Prizes for the winners could be family cookbooks, craft books, or song books.
- *A Simple Cooking Activity* — an activity that requires following a recipe but does not require cooking can be enjoyed by all family members and may inspire them to try to cook together more at home. A handout that includes recipes they can do at home will help parents to see the possibilities for literacy practice that home cooking activities can provide. A math teacher who models measuring and following directions exactly makes a great leader for this activity.
- *A Family Sing Along* — using song sheets, the families sing old favorites together. The music teacher leads this activity, demonstrating how reading can be practiced even when singing.

**Keeping Score**
Keeping Score asks parents to record how their children are reading by putting check marks for each word that the student reads and writing down the words that they missed. The word lists provide mistakes that teachers can analyze for what strategies children are using when they read and what help they still need. Children then win a reward when they correctly read a designated amount of words.

The purpose for this activity is very transparent to both parents and teachers. It provides children with valuable reading time and provides teachers with valuable information. Often, when we ask children to read for 20 minutes a night, we are not sure that they do it unless we require book reports or journals. Younger children especially enjoy reading aloud to their parents, but the bustle of family life does not allow time for reading aloud to other family members. Since this activity provides a direct connection with the teacher on the struggles their children are having, parents see this as a very valuable use of their time and can see the rewards of making time for it.

This family literacy activity, developed by Sharon Pitcher, was first used at Cromwell Valley Elementary School in Towson, Maryland. When children read 1,000 words, they were invited to a special lunch each month. At the end of the school year, their parents were invited to lunch, too. As 1,000 words became easily attainable, the amount of words was increased.

**The Great Poetry Race**
Reading familiar material over and over promotes fluency. In the Great Poetry Race, children are given a poem to read and a form that is signed by anyone the child reads the poem to within a time frame. Groups of students may be given a particular poem that has been selected to practice a skill or strategy being taught to this group. Or, it can be individualized for the students by letting them select a poem. The student who reads the poem to the most people during a specific time frame wins a prize; books make great prizes.

Children and families alike love this activity. Since children are reading to many people, the parents' literacy level does not impact this activity. Children can read the poem over the phone to family members, and the parent can sign the names. They can read to younger sisters and brothers. They can read to neighbors. This activity promotes the school's emphasis on reading and literacy by encouraging participation from members of the community. The librarian again could provide an incredible resource for this activity by developing a large collection of poetry for the teachers to use.

**School-Home Links**
Little Planet Learning developed these activities for the U.S. Department of Education for grades K–3. They are easy phonemic awareness, phonics, and comprehension activities that can be done with any book the children are reading. They can be individualized to meet the needs of groups or individual children. The activities can be printed off the USDE Web site <www.ed.gov/pubs/CompactforReading > or ordered from the Department of Education's EDPUBS distribution center (1-877-433-7827).

**School-Wide Activities**
The following activities are good literacy events for everyone in the school. If the typing and copying of activities is facilitated by the administration, the possibility of all families having the opportunity to do the activities then does not depend on a teacher's time. A school team consisting of teachers, the school librarian, special educators, and reading specialists designs and facilitates activities. Following is an example of a school-wide activity that can be adapted for different school populations and different times of the year.

<table>
<tr><td colspan="3" align="center">**Family Tic Tac Toe**<br><br>**Do three items to make Tic Tac Toe. Bring your completed card into school to put into a raffle.**</td></tr>
<tr>
<td>Read the comics in the newspaper together. Choose one to bring in to class to share.</td>
<td>Cook together reading a recipe. Bring in a sample for your teacher.</td>
<td>Read a picture book together.<br>**Parents Initial Here**</td>
</tr>
<tr>
<td>Make a craft following directions. Bring it in for your teacher to see.</td>
<td>Borrow a cookbook from the library. Bring it in to share with your class.</td>
<td>Search a topic on the Internet that you are interested in. Print what you found to share with your class.</td>
</tr>
<tr>
<td>Read the sports in the newspaper together. Choose one article to bring into class to share.</td>
<td>Make cookies reading a recipe. Bring in a sample for your teacher.</td>
<td>Read an information book together.<br>**Parents Initial Here**</td>
</tr>
</table>

**Figure 4.1:** Family Tic Tac Toe

Using the same principle as the Tic Tac Toe Card (Figure 4.1), a Bingo Card can be made. Activities are done in a row to get "Bingo." Using the Bingo or Tic Tac Toe cards as raffle tickets encourages parents and children to do many activities. Then, a raffle is held with prizes valued by the whole family. In one school, the Bingo card was designed to include holiday activities, such as making cards, wrapping packages using written directions, and making presents. The raffle prize was a package of gift certificates donated by community businesses for the family to enjoy during the Christmas break.

The activities can easily be changed for different age groups. For primary children, the activities can include highlighting sight words in the newspaper, making a list of 10 signs in their neighborhood, or reading nursery rhymes. For older children, reading newspaper ads to find out how to buy an outfit for $50, reading a magazine together, reading about a place, and visiting are all activities that can be included.

# Good Books for Families

Reading aloud at PTA meetings and family activities models for parents the value and the process of engaging children in reading. The following books will help facilitate many memorable opportunities for families:

DeGross, M. (1999). *Granddaddy's Street Songs*. NY: Hyperion Books for Children.
A grandfather tells his grandson about being a vegetable vendor in
Baltimore. A wonderful book for sharing the importance of family stories.

Evans, R.P. (1999). *The Dance*. NY: Simon & Schuster Books for Young Readers.
The story of a father's and daughter's experience over the daughter's lifetime,
centered around dance. Talks about how fathers feel when they watch their
children in different life experiences.

Greenfield, E. (1978). *Honey, I Love and Other Love Poems*. NY: Harper Collins.
Family poems with a special emphasis given to the African-American
experience.

Fox, M. (1988). *Koala Lou*. NY: Voyager Books.
A delightful story of a koala bear and how her mother loves and supports her
throughout many life experiences.

Fox, M. (1997). *Sophie*. NY: Voyager Books.
A child's experience with her grandfather from her birth to his death.

Nolan, J. (1999). *In My Momma's Kitchen*. NY: Lothrop, Lee & Shepard Books.
Stories that celebrate African-American families, and mommas in particular.

Nolan, J. (1998). *Raising Dragons*. NY: Scholastic.
A fanciful tale of a child raising a dragon. Parents can make many connections to her experiences.

Strickland, D.S. (1994). *Families: Poems Celebrating the African American
Experience*. Homesdale, PA: Wordsong.
Wonderful poems for families.

Thomas, J.C. (1998). *Cherish Me*. NY: HarperFestival.
A poem made into a picture book about what a parent cherishes about her
child.

Thomas, J.C. (2001). *Joy*. NY: Hyperion Books for Children.
This is a short board book that celebrates the joy a child brings to a parent.

# Professional Development Ideas

In order for educators to understand the importance of family literacy, it is crucial
that they understand how their own family literacy experiences relate to those of their
students. Some educators are the children of educators or highly educated parents.
They often expect all parents to know how to reinforce education in their homes.
Also, it is sometimes difficult for educators who do not have children to understand
the awesome responsibility that parenting can be in today's world. Another group,
whose backgrounds may get in the way of understanding parents, are those that did
not have parent support as they were growing up. Sometimes they feel that they over-
came the lack of support, so it is not crucial to their students' growth.

Teachers sometimes feel that it is their responsibility to replace the lack of
parental support with increased teacher support. Although this concern is well inten-
tioned, research suggests that reaching out to teach the parent will make the most
impact upon long-term student achievement. One of the following activities may
help your faculty discuss these important issues:

■ Use the questions in the Anticipation Questions at the beginning of the chapter as a needs assessment or reflection at the beginning of a family literacy program or at faculty meetings. The teachers can write their own reflections and then share with other faculty members.

■ Ups and Downs is a great warm-up activity to approach this reflection in a different way. Give these directions: "If your answer to the question is yes, stand up. If your answer is no, sit down." Ask the following questions:

1. Did someone read to you as a child?
2. Did your parents attend school activities on a regular basis?
3. Did your parents take you to the library?
4. Were literacy activities, such as making cards and cooking with recipes, done in your home?
5. Are you a parent?
6. Did you read to your children and take them to the library?
7. Does anyone have grandchildren? Are your children reading to their children and taking them to the library?

As you are doing this, you can stop to have discussions with those standing or sitting. For example, when asking about their parents reading to them and taking them to the library, you could ask if anyone wants to discuss how they felt about their response. A discussion with grandparents is often beneficial to share concerns that young parents today are so busy that they do not have time for literacy activities. This activity brings some important issues to the forefront for discussion. In addition to standing and sitting, the activity can be done with thumbs up and thumbs down or by answering aloud "That's me" for yes.

## Theory Share:

It is extremely important that educators are exposed to family literacy research. Often this topic is not included in teacher education or library science courses. The Exploring the Theory section of this chapter could be used in a professional development session by doing a read-around. Different teachers silently read small parts of the literature review, summarize it, and then share their summaries and lead a group reflection.

Edward's book *A Path to Follow: Learning to Listen to Parents* (1999, Heinemann) provides an excellent resource for a study group on family literacy. The book is easy-to-read (76 pages) and filled with opportunities for reflection and practical application. For example, one of the first activities that she asks teachers to do is write down all of the "fears and hesitations and ways in which you feel you might not be successful and look at what you've written" (p. 24). The activity is a great way to get rid of old prejudices about reaching out to parents. The book also contains eight pages of questions that can be asked of parents to help them talk about themselves and their children, and includes parent stories that resulted from these questions.

## The Practice:

Giving educators time to work in teams to design family literacy activities sets the seeds for collaboration. Including everyone helps the effort reach the whole school. How to reach the hardest-to-reach parents needs to be a priority. After the event is over, a follow-up meeting should be held to evaluate how many parents attended and who they were. Calculate what percentage of all of the parents attended.

Helping school faculties understand the community they are serving is also very important. Edwards (1999) states that many teachers come to the school from other surrounding communities and often never see anything but the road into the school. At the beginning of the school year or while developing your school family literacy program, a bus trip around the community with opportunities to get out at neighborhood restaurants, churches, and libraries can really enrich the teachers' understanding of where their students live. Inviting some of the members of the community to share insights into the community can also give a human face to the neighborhood. Church leaders, preschool directors, store owners, local politicians, and social workers will provide the teachers with a different outlook on their students' lives.

# The Librarian's Link

The school library can be a natural literacy environment for families. The librarian is a potent resource to motivate and encourage family reading. Many low socio-economic areas do not have public libraries, bookstores, or print sources. The school library could be a hub for literacy enrichments after school, evenings, weekends, and summers. Available resources and librarian time are two aspects to be considered when planning family enrichment events within the school library. Extended day and summer time for the librarian needs to be built into the school budget, and more books and materials will be needed for the library to meet the circulation needs this will require.

Neuman & Celano (2001) studied the access to print resources in low-income and middle-income communities and found outstanding differences. Low-income communities did not have bookstores, libraries, magazines in stores, or even many billboards and signs. Little access to reading materials is available to these families, so the school library could offer them so much.

The first step is to provide reading materials for parents as well as for children. Teachers, women's clubs, and churches will often donate inexpensive novels, magazines, and parenting materials if the need is shared with them. Videos are also popular and can be very inexpensive. For example, the I Am Your Child Foundation (<www.iamyourchild.com>) provides $5 videos on infant development, discipline, early literacy, and other topics that can easily be ordered on the Internet. The International Reading Association has a wonderful video on reading to children and inexpensive brochures available through their Web site <www.reading.org >.

Hamilton Elementary School in Memphis, Tennessee, has experimented with a policy that allows families and community members to check out resources from the school library. Thus far, the librarian has experienced few of the anticipated problems, e.g., damaged or lost books, keeping track of patrons, and demand exceeding supply of the desired books, videos, and magazines. In addition, Hamilton school library has brought a variety of community services to the school. Some of these services include storytelling, reading activities, library tours, public Internet connections, and a collaboration with a local television station called Homework Hotline, which helps students and parents complete homework assignments (Maxwell, 2000).

Just setting aside one evening per week for families to gather at the school library can provide many literacy opportunities. Many parents do not have access to computers and would value the opportunity to use the computers with their children. These evenings need very little preparation, but do require trained librarians, not volunteers, who can help parents.

Grants are available to start community outreach programs. Community partners, such as businesses, churches, and community associations, can strengthen grant applications and support these efforts. Stipends or flexible time for school faculty to be available in the evening also facilitates a successful program.

# The Principal's Perspective

A joint project of the National Institute for Literacy and the Planning and Evaluation Service in the Office of the Under Secretary of the U.S. Department of Education provides principals with an important resource for changing home literacy involvement in a school. Following a model from USDE, parents, teachers, librarians, students, and administrators are led through a cognitive process to develop a school "Compact for Reading."

In developing the "Compact for Reading," teachers list what they will do to support the process and what they want administrators and parents to do. Parents complete a similar list, giving them the opportunity to list what they think they should do, and what teachers and administrators should do. A team consisting of teachers, administrators, parents, and community leaders then consolidates these lists. State standards are followed for the expectations for students. At the end of the process, the final document is signed by all of the stakeholders.

Will McKenna, the principal of Waverly Elementary School in Baltimore, Maryland, facilitated this process in his school community during the first year he took over one of the nine lowest performing schools in the state. The parent and teacher discussions helped him understand the needs of his whole school community. The final "Waverly Compact for Reading" is displayed in a prominent place in the school lobby. Parent participation increased, and teacher buy-in to change became apparent. A partnership with Towson University Reading Clinic and CitiFinancial also came out of these discussions. In only two years, this school was taken off the "Failing Schools List," and shows some of the highest gains on standardized test scores in Baltimore City.

For more information on the "Compact for Reading", see the U.S. Department of Education Web site <www.ed.gov >.

# The Collaboration

Fullan (2000), in his work on school reform, suggests that there are at least "five powerful forces that schools must contend with" to improve student achievement.

Parents are one of them. He states, "When parents, the community, the teachers, and the students share a rapport, learning occurs." When all of these groups are working together to focus on literacy, powerful learning enriches everyone.

Often, parents are bombarded with homework and activities that they are expected to do with their children although they do not know the purpose for the activities or have the time to do them. Tension between home and school can result. Family literacy events, coordinated by the librarian, teachers, and the principal, strengthen children/parent literacy interactions, lighten the homework burden for parents, and enable parents and teachers to work together to improve student achievement throughout the school.

This chapter described many different family literacy activities that could be implemented by schools. A common thread that binds the research and the activities in the chapter is the necessity of collaboration to create and facilitate family literacy. Family literacy thus becomes a shared goal of the librarian, the teacher, and the principal. Its value is encouraged and not a burden on any individual literacy stakeholder in a school.

# Reading the Minds of Others

## References

Auerbach, E.R. (1995). Which way for family literacy: Intervention or empowerment. In L.M. Morrow, *Family Literacy: Connections in schools and communities* (p. 11–28). Newark, DE: International Reading Association.

Brizius, J.A. & Foster. (1993). *Generation to generation: Realizing the promise of family literacy*. Ypsilanti, MI: High/Scope Educational Research Foundation.

Bus, A.G., Van Ijzendoorn, M.J., & Pellegrini, A.D. (1995). Joint book reading makes for success in learning to read: A meta-analysis on intergenerational transmission of literacy. *Review of Educational Research, 65* (1), 1–21.

Darling, S. (1994). Literacy is the key. *Education Week, 14* (5).

DeBruin-Perecki, A. and Paris, S.G. (1997). Family literacy: Examining practice and issues of effectiveness. *Journal of Adolescent & Adult Literacy, 40* (8), 596–618.

Dalton, P. & McNicol. (2002). Project brought families to book! *Adult Learning, 13* (7), 7.

Edwards, P.A. (1999). *A path to follow: Learning to listen to parents*. Portsmouth, N.H.: Heinemann.

Fullan, M. (2000). *Three stories of education reform*. Retrieved September 5, 2003, from <http://www.michaelFullan.ca>.

Heath, S.B. (1983). *Ways with words*. New York: Cambridge University Press.

Maxwell, D.J. (2000). Making libraries mobile: Innovation means to give information services greater reach. *Education, 120* (4), 722–730.

Morrow, L.M. (1995). Family literacy: New perspectives, new practices. In L.M. Morrow, *Family Literacy: Connections in schools and communities*. (p. 5–10). Newark, DE: International Reading Association.

Morrow, L.M. (1983). Home and school correlates of early interest in literature. *Journal of Educational Research, 76*, 221–230.

NGA Center for Best Practices (2002). *Family literacy: A strategy for educational improvement*. Retrieved March 1, 2003, from <www.famlit.org/flpp>.

Neuman, S.B. (1997). Family literacy: A social constructivist perspective. Presented at the meeting of the College Reading Association, Boston.

Neuman, S.B. & Caperelli, B.J. (1998). Literacy learning: A family matter. *Reading Teacher, 52* (3), 244.

Neuman, S.B. & Celano, D. (2001). Access to print in low-income and middle-income communities: An ecological study of four neighborhoods. *Reading Research Quarterly, 36* (1), 81.

Neuman, S.B. & Celano, D. (2001). Books aloud: A campaign to 'put books in children's hands.' *Reading Teacher 54* (6), 550.

Padak, N. & Rasinski, T. (1994). *Family Literacy: What is it?* (Occasional Paper #2). Kent: OH: Kent State University. Retrieved March 1, 2003, from <http://literacy.kent.edu/Oasis/fam/inotebook>.

Taylor, D. (1983). *Family literacy: Young children learn to read and write*. London: Heinemann Educational Books.

Taylor, D., & Dorsey-Gaines, C. (1998). *Growing up literate: Learning from inner-city families*. Portsmouth, N.H.: Heinemann.

## Other Resources

IRA Family Literacy Committee (2000). *Family literacy and the school community: A partnership for lifelong learning* (brochure for teachers). Retrieved March 1, 2003, from <www.reading.org>.

IRA Family Literacy Committee (2000). *What is family literacy? Getting involved in your child's literacy learning* (brochure for teachers). Retrieved March 1, 2003, from <www.reading.org>.

Thomas, A.T., Fazio, L., & Stiefelmeyer, B.L. (1999). *Families at school: A guide for educators*. Newark, DE: The International Reading Association.

Thomas, A.T., Fazio, L., & Stiefelmeyer, B.L. (1999). *Families at school: A handbook for parents*. Newark, DE: The International Reading Association.

# Chapter 5

# Real Literacy and Children from Other Cultures

## An Educator's Voice

"Twenty-four nationalities and many more different cultures—these are my students and they all come with their stories! We have the unique ongoing experience of appreciating and exploring each other's culture through the familiar text that is passed from family member to child. We encourage our students and parents to bring their literacy legacy with them and allow our 'family of learners' to grow from each other. Sharing literacy is one of the most important gifts that we have to give each other."

✏ Elementary principal, Clear Creek Independent School District, Texas

## Anticipation Questions

❓ What does real literacy mean for non-English speaking children?
❓ What is bilingual education?
❓ What is ESL (English as a Second Language) education?
❓ Why should second language learners be instructed in reading in their native languages first?
❓ How do the family and communities play a large role in non-English speaking students' quests for real literacy?

## Exploring the Theory

The racial and ethnic diversity of our American children is increasing. In 1999:

■ 65% were white, non Hispanic,
■ 16% were Hispanic,
■ 15% were black, non Hispanic,
■ 4% were Asian or Pacific Islander, and
■ 1% were American Indian or Alaskan Native (Fiore, 2001).

Classrooms with children of various cultures and native languages fill elementary schools. The desire to teach these children to flourish and to succeed in American society has sparked legislation, public policy, and issues of the heart. For example, the International Reading Association not only supports initial literacy instruction in the child's home language but also advocates the right of families to choose the language in which their children receive beginning literacy instruction (IRA, 1998).

Two kinds of instructional approaches exist to teach second language learners. ESL (English as a Second Language) programs focus on assisting LEP (limited English proficient) students acquire the English language. Bilingual education programs advocate that students should learn literacy first in their native language and then transfer that literacy knowledge and skills to English. A person needs to learn to read and write only once. Advocates of bilingual education believe that once learned, the literacy skills and thinking strategies will transfer to a second language unconsciously. Skills such as concepts of print (reading from left to right, top to bottom, and word spacing) and letter-sound associations can easily be transferred. These advocates stress that children learn to read first in the language that they understand best (Cummins, 1989, 2000). Then, instruction within the content areas can be given in English.

For several years, transitional bilingual programs were implemented within most American public school systems. This program transitioned students from their native language to English as soon as possible. Such negative outcomes as replacing both the native language and culture with a new language and culture, not being able to talk with their families, and being ashamed of their native culture led ultimately to not having any language or culture (Golden, 1996).

The developmental bilingual approach is now recognized as a more effective method of teaching second language students. Students stay in this program until they can be literate in both the native language and in English. Students are encouraged to value both the native language and the native culture. The true meaning of bilingualism, two languages and two cultures, is the focus of developmental bilingual programs (Golden, 1996).

Dual Language, or two-way bilingual programs, have attracted much attention recently, especially in school districts in the Southwest. Several variations of this program exist, but essentially, populations of English speakers learn both a new language, i.e., Spanish, and also gradually receive instruction in the new language. The LEP students learn English and gradually receive instruction in English. The goal of a two-way bilingual program is to produce students who are proficient in both languages and can also learn in both languages. Recent studies (Armendariz & Armendariz, 2002; DeJong, 2002; Senesac, 2002) attest to the high student achievement of both language majority and language minority students in such programs.

Regardless of the kind of program used to teach second language learners, two instructional suggestions work well in classrooms. First, recognition of other cultures' values and language (noting traditions on a bulletin board, basic room signs in several languages) affirms diversity instead of promoting 'color blind' classrooms (Nieto, 1999). Using and cherishing several languages provide real world opportunities for multicultural literacy events. Second, a great way to practice English includes classroom conversations, especially when the teacher models questioning and answering strategies.

Building upon the literacy skills that second language learners bring from home affirms both their native language and their culture. The same effective literacy strategies (sequencing, making predictions, retelling) that are taught to English speakers strengthen the LEP student's literacy skills, also. Especially important in closing the gap between test scores of English learners and native English speakers are literacy approaches that specifically focus on vocabulary (McLaughlin, 1993).

# The Practice

Our goals as literacy educators revolve around teaching ESL students to not only function but also excel in our English language and, at the same time, value their sense of cultural identity. Since the explicit teaching of vocabulary is linked to higher test scores for LEP students, strategies that strengthen and improve knowledge of conceptual vocabulary can be easily embedded throughout literacy instruction and literacy interactions in a school.

One such technique is the concept circle. A concept circle allows students to relate words conceptually to one another. Four kinds of concept circles include the following:

■ Fill in all sections of the circle, and then have students name the concept.
■ Shade in a section that does not relate, then name the concept.
■ Leave one or two sections empty, name the concept, and add examples to empty sections.
■ Give students a blank concept circle, have them fill in spaces, and name the concept.

In Figure 5.1, one variation of a concept circle is given; one section does not relate.

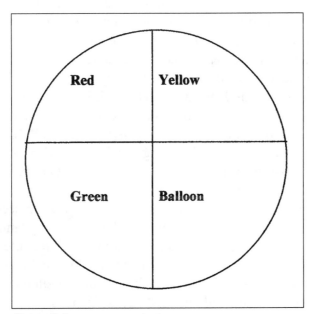

**Figure 5.1:** Concept Circle

Vocabulary instruction results in an increase in word knowledge and reading comprehension. Effective methods of teaching vocabulary include the following:

**1** Information about word meanings,

**2** Use of new word in a variety of contexts, and

**3** Multiple exposures of the new word.

Books and Web sites can be used to help ESL children read English words for words that they know in their own language. This matching can be done through pairing the English word with the word from their language if the children can read in their language. For nonreaders, pictures with the English words are also very effective. The following resources can be helpful in this process:

■ *First Thousand Words* books by Usborne Books <www.ubah.com> come in many different varieties. The books include 1,000 words with the pictures above them. The English version has both a hardbound book and a sticker book with 1,000 stickers with words and pictures that children can use to write stories. A tape and a CD-ROM of the book add interest to those who want technology. Additionally, the book comes in Spanish, French, Russian, Japanese, German, and Italian; all have English translations of the words.

■ A Spanish Picture Dictionary can be found on the Little Explorers Web site <www.littleexplorers.com/languages/Spanishdictionary.html>.

■ The Free Translation Website can be helpful in translating short passages. For a small fee, this site will translate a whole document. Using this technology tool, assessments, such as interest inventories and word lists, can be translated into comparable assessments in the student's first language — <www.freetranslation.com>.

Word walls, bulletin boards, and wall displays throughout a school using a combination of pictures with words in two languages for bilingual schools (and in many languages in diverse culture schools) values cultures and promotes better communication. In the school office, welcome signs in different languages greet parents and children. In the library, organization terms and classifications can be displayed in different languages, promoting an easier access to different materials for all. In classrooms, word walls and bulletin boards in different languages educate and welcome children.

Books in different languages or about different cultures also promote shared understandings. A bilingual librarian is an obvious asset in putting these in place and exposing children to read-alouds in their native language. Books on tape in children's native language promote first language literacy. Displays of these books in the library, in the classrooms, and in the school lobby send an important message to parents that their native languages are valued.

Sharing celebrations from different cultures also can become part of the whole school initiative. Reading about the cultures, inviting families to share food and practices, and making crafts and decorations are all real literacy activities that honor the heritage of different school populations. Multicultural celebrations start with books: resource books for teachers, books for read-aloud and independent reading about the celebrations, and multicultural craft books.

# Professional Development Ideas

Our most valuable multicultural resources are within our schools on a daily basis. The teachers, librarian, other professionals, nonprofessional staff members, and parents constitute a rich, meaningful lesson in multicultural languages, customs, menus, and lifestyles.

## Theory Share:

Nieto (1999) suggests that we have to ask ourselves, "Who does the accommodating?" Are librarians and teachers asking the diverse students and families in schools to accommodate to our ways all of the time? Instead, Nieto suggests that people work for mutual accommodations.

This concept of mutual accommodations can be an important topic of conversation at faculty meetings. Dialogues begin when faculty and staff brainstorm ways that show how all languages and cultures in the school can be valued. How can parents be assisted so they can support their students' learning? Addressing these issues openly at school meetings encourages a valuing of community and cultural bonds.

## The Practice:

In *Going Public* by Shelley Harwayne (1999), she tells the story of Manhattan New School, where 45% of the elementary students come from minority backgrounds. She definitely led all in her school community to be mutually accommodating. The following ideas were used at the Manhattan New School:

1. A wall in the lobby of the school displayed all of the languages of students in the school with the names of the children that spoke that language underneath. When a new student who did not speak English registered in school, teachers, and librarians found another child in the building to translate.
2. Parents were invited to share family portfolios with information about their cultures. Their portfolios were also presented to the faculty.
3. Parents who spoke languages other than English were invited to teach some important words and customs to the teachers.
4. Teachers, librarians, and principals formed study groups to learn more about the cultures of different groups in the school community. (Remember, all speakers of the same language do not have the same culture.)
5. The librarian read aloud a multicultural children's book at each faculty meeting so teachers knew what books were in the school collection for children of other cultures in their rooms.
6. The librarian shared at a faculty meeting the Web sites and books in the previous section so the teachers knew what resources were available for them to understand the languages of their students.

# The Librarian's Link

The impact of student free voluntary reading upon increasing student achievement in language arts has gained much support (Everhart, 2002; Krashen, 1993, 1994). Regardless of which acronym (DEAR-Drop Everything And Read, SSR—Sustained, Silent Reading, etc.) names the free voluntary reading program, several factors (Krashen, 1999) are necessary for one to be successful:

**1** Students have freedom of choice in selecting reading materials.
**2** The physical space should have a print-rich environment.
**3** Students need access to large, library collections.
**4** Time is provided for school-wide free voluntary reading.
**5** Quiet, comfortable places for children to read are always available.
**6** Modeling of reading by parents, friends, teachers, librarians is ongoing.

Obviously, the librarian possesses a crucial role in the effective implementation of a school-wide free voluntary reading program. Purchasing books and other reading materials that will evoke the interests of a diverse, multilingual, and multicultural student and teacher population is simply one avenue through which librarians can foster an atmosphere of respect and tolerance for all our children.

As explained in the "Practice" section of this chapter, the school library can reflect the diverse cultures of the students that it seeks to serve. Having an ESL corner in the library stocked with books that focus on conceptual vocabulary provides a valuable resource to both teachers and students. In addition, cultural variations of the same story, for example, Cinderella (Mikkelsen, 2000), sets the stage for comparisons and contrasts of characters, settings, and cultural values between and among the differing versions of the same story.

# Good Books: Variations on Cinderella

African-American—
   Steptoe, John. (1987). *Mufaro's beautiful daughters*. Lothrop.
American—
   Walt Disney's *Cinderella*. (1986). Western Publishing Company.
American South—
   Hooks, William. (1987). *Moss gown*. Clarion.
Appalachian—
   Chase, Richard. (1948). Ashpet. In *Grandfather tales*. Houghton-Mifflin.
Asian—
   Louie, Ai-Ling. (1982). *Yeh-Shen*. Philomel.
French Creole—
   San Souci, Robert. (1998). *Cendrillon: A caribbean Cinderella*. Simon.

Jewish—
    Jaffe, Nina. (1998). *The way meat loves salt: A Cinderella tale from the Jewish tradition*. Holt.
Middle Eastern—
    Clima, Shirley. (1989). *The Egyptian Cinderella*. Harper.
    Hickox, Rebecca. (1998). *The golden sandal: A middle eastern Cinderella story*. Holiday.
Native-American—
    Rafe, Martin. (1992). *The rough-face girl*. Scholastic.
Norwegian—
    Asbjornsen, P. & Moe, J. (1982). *The Princess on the glass hill*. In Norwegian folk tale. Pantheon.
Vietnamese—
    Lum, Darrell. (1994). *The golden slipper: A Vietnamese legend*. Troll.

# The Principal's Perspective

Principal Emma Armendariz led her New Mexico elementary school through a successful implementation of both a 50/50 and a 90/10 two-way bilingual immersion model. Located in a predominantly Hispanic community in an urban setting, Longfellow Elementary had been designated as a magnet school for Spanish and the fine arts. The original plan included a 50/50 two-way bilingual model. This model means that about half of the student body are English speakers and the other half are non-English speakers. Each student maintains and refines his or her native language while also learning the second language. After a successful implementation of the 50/50 model for one year, the demographics of the student population changed, and this shift caused a necessary change in the bilingual program if it were to meet the needs of the students.

At Longfellow, approximately one-fourth of the entering kindergarten students are monolingual English speakers, one-fourth are monolingual Spanish speakers, and the remaining half are bilingual, ranging from limited to complete fluency in both languages. Instruction for kindergarten and first grade is delivered in a 90/10, Spanish/English ratio. The program attempts to develop the native language for the monolingual English and Spanish speakers, while they also learn a second language.

The primary focus for the bilingual speakers is to recover the language of their heritage and refine their English. Beginning with second grade, the percentage of Spanish used for instruction gradually decreases by 10%. By fifth grade, the language ratio used for instruction has culminated at 50/50, Spanish/English.

This principal attributes the success of this novel two-way bilingual program to her teachers and to the support of the local community. One of the most significant successes, in the view of the principal, is the sense of pride that all of the members of the school community experience when they converse in Spanish and in English (Armendariz & Armendariz, 2002).

# The Collaboration

Throughout the school, welcoming ways can exist to embrace students of diverse cultures. A school librarian versed in multicultural literature and the languages of the school culture can lead this effort. By choosing materials to support these efforts throughout the school, the librarian establishes the library as a hub for multicultural support for the whole school community. Providing library experiences that value different languages and cultures, the librarian leads children to value the heritage of all. Teachers who value cultures in their classrooms and a school environment that welcomes all families support a real literacy school culture that leaves no child or family behind.

Another whole school collaborative idea centers around monthly meetings that focus on a chosen culture. Parents and children who represent the designated culture prepare short conversations, wear native clothing, and provide the menu for the faculty, staff, and parents to bring. All invitations are written in several languages.

This chapter has reviewed the theme of real literacy and how it impacts the educational process of all students, regardless of their native culture or language. As educators strive to meet these challenging needs, such as teaching state curricula to non-English speaking students, collaboration among librarians, teachers, and principals becomes essential to the functioning of a multicultural, multilingual school population.

# Reading the Minds of Others

## References

Armendariz, A. & Armendariz, E. (2002). An administrative perspective of a two-way bilingual immersion program. *Bilingual Research Journal 26* (1), 75–85.

Cummins, J. (1989). *Empowering minority students.* Sacramento, CA: California Association for Bilingual Education.

Cummins, J. (2000). *Language, power, and pedagogy.* Clevedon, UK: Multilingual Matters.

DeJong, E.J. (2002). Effective bilingual education: From theory to academic achievement in a two-way bilingual program. *Bilingual Research Journal 26* (1), 56–64.

Everhart, N. (2002). Long-term tracking of student participants' reading achievement in reading motivation programs. *Knowledge Quest 30* (5), 43–46.

Fiore, C. (2001). Early literacy activities in the USA. Libraries and Librarians: *Making a difference in the knowledge age. Council and general conference: Conference Programme and Proceedings* (67th), Boston, MA.

Golden, John (1996). *Approaches for serving second language learners.* Retrieved May 25, 2003, from <http://www.ncela.gwu.edu/classroom/voices/approach.htm>.

Harwayne, S. (1999). *Going public: Priorities & practices at the Manhattan New School.* Portsmouth, NH: Heinemann.

International Reading Association. (1998). *Second language literacy instruction: A position statement of the International Reading Association.* Online: available at <http://www.reading.org/positions/second_language.html>.

Krashen, S. (1994). The case for free voluntary reading. *Indiana Media Journal 17* (1), 72–82.

Krashen, S. (1993). *The power of reading: Insights from the research.* Englewood, CO: Libraries Unlimited.

Krashen, S. (1999). *Three arguments against whole language and why they are wrong.* Portsmouth, NH: Heinemann.

McLaughlin, B. (1993). *Myths and misconceptions about second language learning: What every teacher needs to unlearn.* Santa Cruz, CA: National Center for Research on Cultural Diversity and Second Language Learning.

Mikkelsen, N. (2000). *Words and pictures: Lessons in children's literature and literacies.* Boston: McGraw-Hill.

Nieto, S. (1999). *Affirming diversity.* New York, NY: Longman Publishing Group.

Senesac, B. (2002). Two-way bilingual immersion: A portrait of quality schooling. *Bilingual Research Journal 26* (1), 65–73.

# Chapter 6

# Real Literacy and Comprehension Instruction

## An Educator's Voice

"Children are taught to read so that they can understand what it is in the text. Thus, most of what matters in reading instruction matters because ultimately it affects whether the student develops into a reader who can comprehend what is in text."

💬 Michael Pressley (2000, p. 545) *Handbook of Reading Research, Volume III*

## Anticipation Questions

*Before beginning this chapter, consider how your present view of comprehension instruction has evolved.*

❓ Take a journey back to your elementary school classroom. How were you taught to comprehend what you read?

❓ What are some of the ways that you have taught comprehension?

❓ How has a child's comprehension influenced your suggestions of books for that child?

❓ What roles do book collection and gradual release of responsibility play in comprehension instruction?

## Exploring the Theory

Many debates have occurred over beginning reading instruction. How should phonics (sounds and letter correspondence) and phonemic awareness (sounds in words) be taught? Often the discussion gets so heated that researchers, librarians, teachers, and principals fail to remember that the point of reading is getting meaning from the text. Getting meaning from what is read is the defining criterion of real literacy. The ultimate goal of instruction associated with reading is having the reader comprehend what is read.

Historically, comprehension was viewed as the process of answering questions or completing workbook pages. In the last third of the 20th century, research on teaching comprehension drastically changed (Pearson, 2002). We learned how the mind processes text and how we can share this process with children. We also learned what good librarians for decades knew: choosing the right book or reading material matters.

In order to comprehend text, children have to be able to read the words and understand what they mean (Pressley, 2000). The good reader does not read sound by sound but chunks a word into meaningful units. For example, the good reader would read the word "unfaithful" as un (meaning not), faith (meaning belief), ful (meaning having lots of). The reader would conclude that the unfaithful wife can not be trusted. Chunking a word into meaningful units represents the first level of understanding in the comprehension process.

After words are identified, the reader then goes through an automatic process of connecting, thinking, choosing, and making sense. Connections are more easily made when the reader is able to bring experiences and a sense of language to the text. As readers are reading, they acquire meaning, confirm meaning, or create meaning. In summary, "reading comprehension is the process of meaning making" (Gambrell, Block, & Pressley, 2002, p. 5).

Good librarians and teachers realize that comprehension does not happen without motivation. Good comprehenders not only have the skills to read but they want to read (Gambrell, 2001). This will to read needs to be intrinsic. The reader must want to read and must see a personal benefit in the process. This belief is sometimes forgotten when children are all forced to continually read the same book or materials.

The act of comprehending has three important components: the reader, the text, and the activity (Sweet & Snow, 2002). First, who the readers are (their experiences) defines how they come to the text. Second, the text itself either encourages or limits comprehension. The child who is reading a difficult book about a topic that doesn't interest him will comprehend less than the child who is reading an appropriately matched book about his favorite topic. Finally, the reason the reader is reading this particular text is important. Often, when a child is reading the text for someone else's (the teacher's or the school's) purposes, comprehension lessens.

The sociocultural context is also crucial to reading comprehension (Sweet & Snow, 2002). Where the child reads and how the society that is important to the child views reading also affect comprehension. A child comprehends better in a relaxed classroom context where she has a choice of sitting on a sofa, lying on a rug on the floor, or resting in a chair by the window. The traditional classroom with desks in a row with the child sitting up straight with her feet on the floor gives little consideration to the learning needs of the reader. A child who has been read to, values reading, and is encouraged to read by significant adults in his life more actively comprehends during the reading process.

Researchers (Pearson, 2002; Pressley, 2000) over the last 20 years have come to realize that reading is a metacognitive process. Readers think about how they are thinking when they are reading. When we teach the process of our thinking (metacognition) to students, their comprehension increases.

Research on metacognitive theories states that when good readers are reading, they are using the following processes:

- Activating prior knowledge and *making connections* to what they know,
- *Determining* the most important *ideas* in their reading,
- Asking *questions to clarify* or focus their understanding,
- Creating *visual images* of what the words are saying,
- *Inferencing* or creating meaning as they read,
- *Synthesizing* what is read to create a unified message for themselves of what the reading means, and
- Utilizing different strategies to *fix up* any confusion they have when they are reading. These *fix-up strategies* can occur in any part of the process (reading the words, understanding the words, transforming the words into meaning) (Keene, 2002; Keene & Zimmerman, 1997).

Teaching reading comprehension works best in a context that values the needs of the student. Gradual release of responsibility (explained in chapter 2) is the key. The strategies have to be explicitly taught, modeled, and nurtured through repeated opportunities for application, with teacher coaching and with many varying opportunities for approximation. Most important, comprehension builds when students apply strategies independently when they read.

In a study done by Block (Gambrell, Block & Pressley, 2002) with elementary school students, children were randomly assigned to control and experimental groups. The experimental group was taught reading strategies for 32 weeks using a gradual release of responsibility approach as described here. The experimental group outperformed the control group (who was not taught the strategies) on both standardized tests and in demonstrations of the strategies outside of school.

Opportunities in schools for students to read independently have been found to be crucial for these strategies to become automatic for students. All kinds of reading material that are on the child's level and are easily accessible are a necessity for developing comprehension skills. Giving children the opportunities to read in school for enjoyment has always been a passionate plea by librarians and has now been suggested by researchers to make the biggest difference for struggling readers (Allington, 2001).

Duke and Pearson (2001) suggest that in addition to opportunities to read, automaticity in decoding, and strategy instruction, the following items are essential for effective comprehension instruction:

- An environment rich in high-quality talk about text, and
- Lots of time writing texts for others to understand (p. 3).

These two topics, conversations and writing, will be addressed separately in Chapters 7 and 8.

# The Practice

When teaching comprehension skills, scaffolding the instruction is very important. To increase student literacy achievement, teach one strategy at a time until students have internalized it. It may take weeks to teach one strategy, but the students will learn it for life. Students who learn a strategy this way will use it when they read silently and when they take tests. When teachers in different subject areas collaborate to teach the same strategy, the result is very powerful.

**The following procedure outlines the steps to teaching a strategy in a gradual release manner:**

**1** Explain the strategy in explicit terms and make a chart explaining its use and importance.

**2** Model the strategy by reading aloud and stopping at major places throughout the book to demonstrate using the strategy.

**3** Have the students practice the strategy together in a shared reading. The teacher questions and coaches as they practice.

**4** Give the students multiple opportunities to practice the strategy with support—small guided reading groups, literacy centers, and at home. Give support when needed until they are applying the strategy independently.

**5** In teaching the strategies, use devices that are real. For example, visual organizers are often important for a child who learns by seeing. Choose visual organizers carefully. Dittos are usually not effective approaches. When children are independently reading a novel on their own, are they going to have a ditto to fill out? Instead, teach them to use their hand as the organizer. The thumb is the beginning of the story, the next finger is the middle, the next the end, the next the setting, and the next the characters.

**6** Having students make a plastic, disposable retelling glove is another way to teach this strategy. Write the words "beginning," "middle," "end," "setting," and "characters" on the fingers of the glove with a permanent marker. Whenever they retell a story, they use the glove to help them remember the different components of retelling. When this strategy has been internalized, remove gloves, and students will remember the different components of retelling just by looking at their hands.

**7** Sticky notes are another great device for helping students comprehend. Many uses for sticky notes are the following:

* Writing questions to clarify what is being read. As the readers find the answers in further reading, they find and answer their own questions.
* Making little notes throughout the reading, writing connections they have with the text.
* Determining importance by identifying key words in the text as they are reading. After they read, they can use the key words to retell the story.

The strategies are often taught in the following order (listed from developmentally easiest to hardest):

**1** *Making Connections* — children can easily understand how to connect what they are reading to themselves, or to other books they have read, or to the world in which they live. All possible connections to text should be taught so that children can see the many ways they can connect with what they read. These connections are also important to activate the prior knowledge of the reader.

**2** *Questioning* — good readers ask themselves questions when they read to clarify the reading and to predict what is going to happen next. Since children are naturally comfortable with asking questions, this strategy is easy for them to internalize.

**3** *Fix-up Strategies* — it is important to help students monitor their own comprehension and to understand when it breaks down. These strategies lead children to ask themselves, "Does this make sense; does it look right?" Soon they will begin to develop their own strategies, like re-reading the sentence, when they want to understand the text. Since many children do not naturally monitor their reading for meaning, knowing how to use fix-up strategies is essential for comprehension.

**4** *Determining Importance* — traditionally we have always taught children to figure out the main idea of what they read. Determining importance is the same skill but on a bigger scale. Whenever we read, we are determining importance by choosing what we need to remember to make meaning.

**5** *Visualizing* — many good readers see pictures in their head when they read. Guiding children to develop this strategy often helps with their remembering all of the strategies and is especially important for a visual learner. Helping children draw their visual understandings of the story is fun and often activates their natural process to visualize.

**6** *Inferring* — understanding the implicit or subtle meanings of text is a very hard skill for most children. What is not being said? What is the underlying meaning? Many children need weeks of scaffolding and independent applications to master this elusive strategy.

**7** *Synthesizing* — represents the completion skill in reading comprehension. Synthesizing requires taking what was learned from all of the other strategies, putting all the meanings together, and producing new levels of understanding.

# A Scaffolding Map for Teaching the Skill of Questioning

**Day 1:** As the teacher reads aloud to the children, she models different ways of asking questions about the text. The text is marked where the teacher stops reading. After the demonstration, the teacher explains why it is important to ask questions in our head when we read. She asks the children to tell some questions about the text. After writing students' questions on a chart, she gives the students the opportunity to read aloud with a partner and to ask questions.

**Day 2:** The teacher again models the strategy of questioning as she reads aloud, but this time she writes her questions on sticky notes. Students are given the opportunity to use sticky notes as they read aloud with a partner.

**Day 3:** The teacher models the questioning strategy again by writing questions on sticky notes as she reads aloud. When she has finished the book, she tries to answer her questions with the book closed. The teacher then lets the students practice this strategy in small groups. The teacher may choose to lead some of the groups if the children need extra coaching. In the groups without the teacher, the children coach each other.

**Day 4:** The teacher reads poems, paragraphs, and so on from the overhead projector. The teacher assists the children to read together in a shared reading experience. She writes in the side margins of the transparency questions that the students have asked. Children then read additional poems to choose one with which to use this strategy. Children then find another child who read the same poem, and they compare their questions.

**Days 5–10:** At the different literacy centers within the classroom, children choose materials to read as they apply the questioning strategy. The teacher constantly monitors each child's progress as each is observed using the strategy. While working in small groups for instructional purposes (guided reading groups), she coaches students about applying this strategy. She continues to begin the instructional period with a short, modeling mini-lesson when she reads aloud. If a child has not yet mastered the application of the strategy, she provides individual assistance.

**Days 11–15:** Using the assistance of the school librarian or content area teachers, the teacher seeks to see if the children are applying the strategies whenever they read. This step is crucial because children often will do something when the teacher is present but not realize that it should be applied to all reading. If children apply the strategy in other classrooms, they will apply it on standardized tests and in real literacy settings.

# Professional Development Ideas

Leading the faculty to see how they use comprehension strategies when they read is one of the best ways to introduce this concept. Comprehension strategies were gathered from research that involved observing and documenting exactly what good readers do as they read. Many teachers use these strategies when they personally read, so professional development that links how teachers read with how students read provides crucial insights.

Following are some questions that will spark a discussion:

- How many times have you taught reading strategies to children but you don't see them apply the strategies when they are taking a standardized test? What do you need to do differently?
- What is the average amount of time that you spend teaching one strategy?
- What strategies do good readers use? Do you use these when you read?

In answering these questions, the faculty is led to discuss their own metacognitive strategies. Listing the strategies on a chart or pairing up to share responses allows the faculty to reflect on the use and teaching of comprehension strategies.

## Theory Share:

Choose a book that provokes thought and even debate. Ahead of time mark some provocative parts with sticky notes to remind yourself to stop at this point for thinking. Read it aloud once to the teachers so that they hear the whole story (a model for good practice). Then re-read it, stopping about four or five times. When you pause, ask them to jot down on a piece of paper what they are thinking at this place in the story.

After you are finished reading, put up a chart or an overhead with the following symbols on it:

? Questions
& Connections
^ Inferring
$ Visualizing
# Synthesizing
% Determining Importance

Ask the teachers to look at their reflections and code them with these different symbols according to the strategies they used. Check to see by a show of hands how many teachers used all of the strategies. Determine which strategy was used the most times. Recent research in comprehension instruction suggests that these six strategies are the most important ones that a reader uses to make meaning from text. The faculty can also list strategies from the easiest to the hardest and discuss their reasons for their sequence.

At the end of the professional development session, it is important to refer back to the questions that were asked at the beginning of the session. Discuss the amount of time it takes to learn a strategy and why children sometimes do not apply strategies both on tests and in their everyday readings. Then, discuss how much time should be spent on one strategy using the gradual release of responsibility framework. Share the "Scaffolding Map for Teaching Questioning" in the earlier part of this chapter.

## The Practice:

A wonderful way to quickly get this type of comprehension instruction into a school is to assign each grade level a strategy to teach across the whole grade level. The teachers can work together to plan the mini lessons. The content area teachers can use the strategy in their classrooms, too. The librarian is given the time to sit in on all of the grade level meetings so she can reinforce the strategies in her library instruction and assess whether she sees the children independently using the strategies when they come to the library. All instruction involving reading revolves around this one strategy for at least a two- to three-week period of time.

The librarian plays a key role in this effort by suggesting books for read-alouds across grades and curriculum, and models for the whole group an interactive read aloud. Read-alouds using the strategy could be done in all areas of instruction (the library, the gym, art, computers, social studies, science, and music), but many content area and classroom teachers may not know how to make read-alouds engaging. Librarians have the most experience and expertise in read-alouds and could take the leadership in this professional development. All members of the school team can share this responsibility to help the children apply a strategy to independence, the final stage of comprehension instruction. The classroom teacher takes the lead in introducing the instruction, but the other faculty members reinforce the instruction by using read-alouds and observing if students apply the strategy independently.

# Good Books for Teaching Strategies

Leavitt, M.J. (1995). *A Snow Story*. New York: Simon & Schuster.
> This book is good to use for the professional development activity. It presents a thought-provoking story about a man who writes poems in the snow. Many places in the story require higher levels of comprehension to understand the language and the concepts.

Dakos, K. (1993). *Don't Read This Book Whatever You Do!* New York: Simon & Schuster.
> This humorous book of poetry can be used for making connections, questioning, synthesizing, and visualizing. The author, a former fifth grade teacher and reading specialist, portrays poems about funny school occurrences.

Cannon, J. (1997). *Verdi*. New York: Harcourt Brace & Co.
> This story about a snake growing up is a wonderful text to teach synthesis and inferencing.

Perdomo, W. (2002). *Visiting Langston*. New York: Henry Holt and Co., LLC.
> This book provides great pieces of text for determining importance with an important point surrounded by supportive text cradled on every two-page spread.

Our 8th graders have designed a float and need your vote!

What to vote for:

"Truest Friendship" by Lang Middle School

SpongeBob and Friends Float

How to vote:

During the parade, each float will display a unique number provided by AT&T that will allow callers to register their votes via text message. Voting will also be conducted at the Co-merica Bank New Year's Parade website: www.comericabankparade.com.

Voting will begin at 2:30 p.m. on January 1, 2010 and conclude at 11:59 p.m. on January 2, 2010. Televised on Fox 4 in Dallas. The winner will be announced on January 8, 2010.

Thanks for your support!

...se to model the comprehension strategies, ...as literacy leaders. A special area of the ...books for modeling the six strategies. ...r different student reading levels that are ...As the teachers use the books, they could ...dea of where to pause in the book or a mini ...d the book.

...look for in books that teach the six strategies:

...ught-provoking opportunities. ...and characters that are easily identifiable with

...otle meanings or abstract understandings. ...escriptions so that the words lead the reader to

...mposed of many different incidents. ...iction books with rich detail.

...k (Harvey & Goudvis, 2000) contains an ... each comprehension strategy (p. 197–206). Another resource is *Matching Books to Readers* (Fountas & Pinnell, 1999), which lists the level of reading difficulty of thousands of books.

# The Principal's Perspective

Cindy Stamps, principal of McWhirter Professional Development Lab School in Houston, Texas, represents the new breed of "literacy principals" (Booth & Rowsell, 2002). At monthly faculty and staff meetings on Wednesday afternoons, Cindy models a literacy strategy that her teachers can replicate in their classrooms. To emphasize comprehension strategies, especially making connections, she demon-strates a read-aloud of *Yay, You: Moving Out, Moving Up, Moving On* (Boynton, 2001). Before she reads, an anticipation guide is shown. This anticipation guide is composed of four statements that may or may not describe the professional goals of her teachers and other professional staff members. Each person reflects on each statement and decides if that statement describes his or her professional goals and vision. Cindy reads the story, stopping at important points to allow and encourage discussion. After the book is finished, faculty and staff share in small groups how their view of themselves in terms of their professional goals was changed by this book. They also discuss how they could use what Cindy modeled in their class-rooms. Some teachers even used it the next day.

Elementary principals, such as Cindy Stamps, recognize the necessity of literacy leadership to raise student achievement scores and develop exemplary teaching. They read the research, study the practice, and model it for their faculty.

Booth and Rowsell (2002) suggest that principals lead their schools to create a literacy-based framework with an achievable, shared vision by everyone working together "to examine teaching practices, explore new ideas, set priorities, establish shared goals, decide on tasks and determine who will complete them" (p. 10). They also suggest that the principal involve all stakeholders in this whole-school initiative and make sure that all "receive credit for their efforts" (p. 10). Comprehension instruction could provide a starting point for this type of collaboration.

## The Collaboration

From his studies of exemplary teachers, Allington (2001) states that if he were going to "establish guidelines for quantity" of books, he would suggest that every classroom have 500 different books, including an equal amount of fiction and non-fiction titles. To effectively teach comprehension strategies, libraries and classrooms need books on many varying reading levels, books about many varying topics, and books that represent many varying cultures. Children need books that they can connect with, find importance in, and question. Teachers need books to use for read-alouds to demonstrate the strategies. This task becomes possible when the school librarian oversees this goal for the whole school, buying the books at discount prices and rotating them to meet the needs of both instruction and children. Classroom teachers are often overwhelmed by this suggestion of a vast collection of a variety of books, but the expertise of the librarian can make this "impossible" task become a reality.

Giving students lots of opportunities to apply reading strategies in books of their choice is crucial for strategies to become intrinsic. When strategies are intrinsic, achievement gains in test scores occur in schools. Reading researchers suggest that the best investment in elementary schools to increase student achievement is to buy as many books as you can.

Encouraging faculty investment in reading revolves around collaboration and ownership of a literacy-based framework. Comprehension instruction can provide a vehicle for this collaboration. Read-aloud demonstrations of a strategy can be done in the library as well as the classroom. The librarian and content area teachers could provide important information to the classroom teacher about whether children are independently applying strategies whenever they read. All of this begins by providing time and opportunities for the whole school faculty to meet, examine instructional needs, and plan.

As suggested by Booth and Rowsell (2002), the principal sets the stage for this collaboration to happen. She or he knows the research and is willing to model as Cindy Stamps did. She understands and acknowledges the expertise that each faculty member brings to this collaboration (such as having the librarian demonstrate read-alouds and lead in the purchasing of books to support the instruction). If a realistic amount of time is also factored in to allow for collaboration, the resulting increase in student achievement and real literacy skills in children will be celebrated by all.

# Reading the Minds of Others

## The Research

Allington, R.L. (2001). *What really matters for struggling readers: Designing research-based programs.* New York: Longman.

Booth, D. & Rowsell, J. (2002). *The literacy principal: Leading, supporting, and assessing reading and writing initiatives.* Ontario, Canada: Pembroke.

Boynton, S. (2001). *Yay, you: Moving out, moving up, moving on.* New York: Simon and Schuster.

Duke, N.K. & Pearson, P.D. (2001). Effective Practices for Developing Reading Comprehension. Retrieved February 7, 2003, from <http://edwev3.educ.msu.edu/wev3.educ.msu.edu/pearson/pdppaper/Duke/ndpdp.html>.

Keene, E.O. (2002). From good to memorable: Characteristics of highly effective comprehension teaching. In C.C. Block, L.B. Gambrell, M. Pressley (Eds.), *Improving reading instruction: Rethinking, research, theory, and classroom practice* (p. 80–105). San Francisco: Jossey-Bass.

Keene, E.O. & Zimmerman (1997). *Mosaic of thought: Teaching comprehension in a reader's workshop.* Portsmouth, NH: Heinemann.

Gambrell, L.B.; Block, C.C., & Pressley, M. (2002). Introduction: Improving comprehension: An urgent priority. In C.C. Block, L.B. Gambrell, M. Pressley (Eds.). *Improving reading instruction: Rethinking, research, theory, and classroom practice.* San Francisco: Jossey-Bass.

Pearson, P.D. (2002). American Reading Instruction Since 1967. In N.B. Smith, *American reading instruction: Special edition.* Newark, DE: The International Reading Association.

Pressley, M. (2000). What should comprehension instruction be the instruction of? In M.L. Kamil, P.B. Mosenthal, P.D. Pearson, and R. Barr (Eds.). *Handbook of reading research: Volume III.* Mahwah, NJ: Lawrence Erlbaum Assoc.

Sweet, A.P. & Snow, C. (2001). Reconceptualizing reading comprehension. In C.C. Block, L.B. Gambrell, M. Pressley (Eds.), *Improving reading instruction: Rethinking, research, theory, and classroom practice* (p. 80–105). San Francisco: Jossey-Bass.

## The Practice

Fountas, I.C. & Pinnell, G.S. (1999). *Matching books to readers: Using leveled books in guided reading, K–3.* Portsmouth, NH: Heinemann. (This resource lists the reading level of thousands of books for young children.)

Harvey, S. & Goudvis, A. (2000). *Strategies that work: Teaching comprehension to enhance understanding.* York, ME: Stenhouse. (Includes several mini-lessons for many levels of students and a list of children's literature that could be used to teach each strategy.)

Holt, L. (1999). *Revisit, reflect, retell: Strategies for improving reading comprehension.* Portsmouth, NH: Heinemann. (Simple lessons and visual organizers for teaching strategies.)

Holt, L. (2000). *Snapshots: Literacy mini lessons up close.* Portsmouth, NH: Heinemann. (More wonderful mini-lessons.)

# Chapter 7

# Conversations for Real Literacy

## An Educator's Voice

"I was amazed to see how motivated these students were when we gave them choices on books to read for the book clubs. They were so engaged and enthusiastic. The students, who were normally behavior problems, were absolute angels in this environment. When time came for book club discussions, all the students had their materials read, responses written, and were prepared to discuss the night's reading because they had chosen the book."

💬 A teacher participating in a summer school enrichment program in Baltimore, Maryland

## Anticipation Questions

❓ How does conversation impact real literacy?
❓ In your classroom, how much of the time do you talk, and how much of the time do the children talk?
❓ Have you ever participated in a book club?
❓ Have you ever bought a book after hearing others talk about it?
❓ What part does conversation play in authentic literacy assessments?

*In this chapter, read about the important role that discussion plays in children's literacy development.*

## Exploring the Theory

Fullan (2001) suggests that an important key to educational change in a school is looking at how actively engaged students are in "constructing their own meaning and learning" (p. 162). Billings and Fitzgerald (2002) describe many examples in the research to support how difficult it is for teachers to move away from "teacher fronted" talk to student-centered discussion. Student-centered discussion is crucial to student engagement and literacy development. Student literacy conversations in the classroom not only deepen students' understanding of the texts but they also influence what students think about reading itself.

Almasi (1996) concludes from much of her research that most of the discussion that goes on in classrooms is more "recitation" talk in which teachers ask questions that have a predetermined answer. This type of talk does not foster student interaction or text meaning construction. Through conversing in the classroom, students are forced both to construct meaning by transacting with the text and to share reflections with those that they are conversing with at the time. Almasi (1996) believes that it is in these more in-depth transactions with the text and others that "new understandings and meanings may emerge" (p. 6).

Through research that was focused on improving learning in schools, the Institute for Learning at the University of Pittsburgh developed nine Principles of Learning. One of the important principles, *Accountable Talk*, has been adopted in many literacy programs across the country. According to the Institute of Learning (2001), "Talking with others about ideas and work is fundamental to learning" (p. 1). For classroom talk to promote learning, it needs to be accountable "to the learning community, to accurate and appropriate knowledge, and to rigorous thinking" (p. 1).

Conversation of this type does not happen naturally in a classroom but must be scaffolded by the teacher. The teacher teaches appropriate responses, demands rigorous support for statements made, "rejoices" when levels of talk challenge thinking, and finds ways to encourage more student-to-student conversations than teacher-to-student and student-to-teacher ones. Conversations in literacy classrooms promote a learning community that is engaged, thinking, stretching, and growing through words.

Peterson & Eeds (1990) define a type of conversation often used in literacy-based classrooms as "grand conversations." Grand conversations are discussions where children share their responses to reading materials, the connections that they make, their predictions, and their questions. The talk is free flowing among the students with the teacher as another participant, not a leader, in the dialogue.

Literacy conversations in classrooms emerged from the movement to bring literature discussion groups into classrooms. Literature circles, often called book clubs, promote discussion within small groups of students who have chosen a common book. The students have a *choice* to read one of six or seven books chosen by the teacher. Students set their assignments and their agenda for discussions. In addition, students collaborate on the design and completion of a project that reflects an aspect of their chosen book. Students complete written responses to the readings to help them to participate more fully in the discussions. Research on literature circles/discussion groups suggests that the discussion process promotes deeper student thinking and learning (Peterson & Eeds, 1990; Raphael & McMahon, 1994).

A good indicator of whether a classroom is literacy-based is the amount and kind of conversations happening in the room. Real literacy conversation reflects the engagement of the learners and the understanding of the teacher that his role is one that facilitates deep thought and not simple answers. As educators visiting a classroom, should we value the very quiet room that we remember of our youths? No, we celebrate the room that buzzes with talk reflecting students' understandings that they are accountable as a member of a learning community to communicate and listen.

# The Practice

From the beginning of a child's school career, teachers encourage talk in the classroom. The preschool and kindergarten classrooms are full of oral language experiences:

- Finger rhymes ("Where is Thumbkin?"; "Eensy, Weensy Spider"),
- Songs (Raffi's "Down by the Bay", "Go Tell Aunt Rhody").
- Show and tell,
- Conversations at center time,
- Repetitious songs ("Roll Over", "Old McDonald Had A Farm"), and
- Nursery rhymes ("Wee Willie Winkie", "Humpty Dumpty").

For many children, their first exposure to the rhythm and patterns of oral language is hearing traditional Mother Goose nursery rhymes. The amount of words known and the understanding of sounds in words contribute to how well a child learns to read. Instruction in early childhood classrooms should include interactive read-aloud, word play, and lots of chances for children to talk to each other.

## Interactive Read-Aloud

Reading aloud exposes children to the excitement and joy that reading can be and models for them what good readers do. In interactive read-aloud, teachers choose a few dynamic places to stop in the book to give the children a chance to talk about the story. This step is an art. Choosing too many places to stop detracts from the story. Allowing lengthy conversations also stops the flow of the story and lessens the ability for children to remember the theme. Find a few choice places in the book where children can make connections to the story. Pose a provocative question to encourage the children to think and talk. Letting the conversation flow from child to child begins a sense of dialogue among the students. About three conversations during a 20-page book are appropriate. Discussion at the end flows naturally, too.

*Great Teacher Resource for Read-Alouds:*
   *Read-Alouds with Young Children* by Campbell (2001)

## Accountable Talk

The Institute for Learning at the University of Pittsburgh coined the term, *Accountable Talk*. This practice demands that students realize that their classroom talk has to be accountable to the following:

- Their learning community,
- The portrayal of accurate information,
- The ability to supply evidence for their claims, and
- The realization that they need to take time to think before talking (Institute for Learning, 2001, p. 1).

In understanding the importance of the learning community, the students are led to realize that they have an obligation to listen and participate. They are encouraged to talk to each other and not just the teacher. Listening and valuing the conversations of others are taught through body language, active interchanges, and connecting each occasion of talk to one that comes before. Talk that is inappropriate or not valuing of others in the learning community is discouraged. Peer pressure discourages talking without thinking first.

The students are also held accountable for accurate information. They are taught to ask clarifying questions if information is not clear. They are taught to challenge peers who shared inaccurate information.

Students are expected to support and give evidence for all of their opinions. Reactions to reading should be followed with "I felt this way because..." Students are also encouraged to challenge their peers with statements such as, "Can you justify ..." or "I need clarification of..." or "Can you give me an example of ..."

Teachers who utilize *Accountable Talk* in their classrooms actively teach the procedures. Initiating the strategy usually starts with charting appropriate sentence stems and inappropriate responses. Some examples given by the Institute for Learning (2001) as appropriate sentence beginners are the following:

- I believe ... because ...
- In my opinion ...
- I agree with ...
- I need clarification ...
- Could you justify ...

***Great Teacher Resource for Accountable Talk:***
*The Institute for Learning Web site* <www.instituteforlearning.org>

## Grand Conversations

Grand Conversations naturally flow from a read-aloud or any shared reading experience. The students experience the reading, whether it is read to them, they read together (shared reading), or they read it themselves. Time is given for each child to write down ideas (more about ways to write in response to texts is presented in Chapter 8). Children share ideas and focus conversations upon others' responses.

To facilitate these conversations, environments are crucial. By sitting comfortably in a circle on a rug, students have opportunities to look at one another as they talk. Conversations flow naturally. Sitting in rows in desks often detracts from the free-flow of ideas.

The teacher's role in the conversation is to begin dialogues using simple open-ended questions, such as, "What did you think about the beginning of this book?" Teachers rehearse the procedures for Grand Conversations before students begin this strategy. This procedure involves:

**1** Each child contributes something to the conversation before another child can add a second comment.

**2** Children ask clarifying questions, such as, "Why did you decide that?" "Can you show me in the book where that happened?" or "Can you give me some examples from the book?"

The key for Grand Conversations is to guide students to value one another's ideas and to listen carefully enough to ask questions.

As children become proficient with this procedure, the teacher's role in the conversation lessens. It is essential to encourage children to talk to each other and not to her. Grand Conversations consist of student-to-student talk and not student-to-teacher interchanges. This strategy promotes deeper thinking after reading and gives children the opportunities to practice and to observe peers as they model all of the major reading strategies.

## Accountable Talk Throughout a Literacy-Based School

Accountable talk is not used exclusively in a language arts classroom. If literacy instruction evolves from collaboration, the same accountable talk stems could be used throughout the school. If all of the faculty (classroom teachers, content teachers, librarians, and administrators) have shared expectations that children will support opinions, clarify answers, and react to one another's talk, children will learn the role talk plays in literacy. Use of talk as letting children share with a partner before a whole group discusses a topic can increase the engagement of children in any class.

*Great Teacher Resource for Grand Conversations:*
    *Grand Conversations: Literature Groups in Action* by Peterson & Eeds (1990)

## Literature Circles and Book Clubs

Grand conversations often happen in literature circles and book clubs. In literature circles children read the same book (on emergent and early reading levels, students will be reading picture books), and then they discuss the book. In book clubs, the children are usually reading chapter books and following the same procedure. Characteristics of both literature circles and book clubs:

- Books are chosen so a class can be divided into small groups of about five students (five groups/five different books/25 students).
- Each student chooses the book she wants to read and thus self-selects her group.
- Groups meet and plan a schedule to read the book.
- Students in the groups also choose topics and questions that interest them.
- All group members read the book and write down their responses to the questions and topics.
- Students discuss the book.
- Students usually develop a final project that presents the book to the rest of the class.

*Literature Circles and Book Clubs in the Library,*
*Social Studies, and the Art Room*
Literature circles also do not have to be confined to the language arts classroom. Imagine the excitement of children looking forward to coming to the library to meet with their book club. Consider conversations in the art room if children are in book clubs to look at the work of illustrators and then share what they see. Reading historical fiction to support the study of a historical period could enhance social studies.

*Book Club: A Literature-Based Curriculum, Second Edition* (Raphael, Pardo, & Highfield, 2002).

*Literature Discussion Groups in the Middle Grades* (Evans, 2001)

# Good Books for Literature Circles and Book Clubs

### Kindergarten–1st grade

*A Chair for My Mother*, Vera Williams, (Greenwillow, 1982)

*Alexander and the Terrible, Horrible, No Good, Very Bad Day*, Judith Viorst, (Simon & Schuster, 1972)

*Amber Brown is Not a Crayon*, Paula Danziger, (Putnam, 1984)

*Amelia Bedelia*, Peggy Parish, (Harper Collins, 1969)

*And to Think that I Saw it on Mulberry Street,* Dr. Seuss, (1937, New York: Random House)

*Goodnight Moon*, Margaret Wise Brown, (Harper & Row, 1947)

*Little Blue and Little Yellow,* Leo Lionni, (Morrow, William, and Company, 1994)

*The Mitten,* Jan Brett, (Putnam, 1989)

*The Polar Express*, Chris Van Allsburg, (Houghton-Mifflin, 1985)

*The Velveteen Rabbit*, Margery Williams, (Godine, David, 1973)

*Where the Wild Things Are*, Maurice Sendak, (Harper & Row, 1963)

### 2nd–4th grade

*Sarah, Plain and Tall*, Patricia MacLachlan, (Harper & Row, 1985)

*The Legend of the Bluebonnet: An Old Tale of Texas*, Tomie dePaulo, (Putnam, 1983)

*The Lion, the Witch, and the Wardrobe*, C.S. Lewis, (Macmillan, 1961)

*Pink and Say*, Patricia Polacco, (Putnam, 1994)

### 5th–6th Grade

*Harry Potter and the Sorcerer's Stone*, J. K. Rowling, (Scholastic, 1997)

*My Side of the Mountain*, Jean George, (Penguin Putnam, 1988)

*Number the Stars*, Lois Lowry, (Houghton Mifflin, 1990)

*Tuck Everlasting*, Natalie Babbit, (Farrar, Strauss, and Giroux, 1977)

# Professional Development Ideas

One of the best ways to help faculty members understand the power of conversations as a means of enhancing text understandings is to have them share in the experience. Faculty book clubs can be a powerful way to engage in conversations and to deepen everyone's knowledge of literacy. Through these clubs, the concepts of Grand Conversations and Accountable Talk can also be shared.

Getting your faculty started with book clubs can happen by:

■ Brainstorm professional books about literacy instruction that the faculty would like to read.

- Form several groups; each group read2 one of the selected books.
- All group members read the books.
- Model the concepts of Grand Conversations and Accountable Talk.
- Describe procedures for literature circles and book clubs.
- Plan an extended period of time for groups to collaborate.
- Each group presents to the whole group at the end.

### *Great Resource to Start Faculty Book Clubs*

The International Reading Association has developed materials for Literacy Study Groups. On each theme there is a module that includes a facilitator guide, at least one professional book, articles from IRA resources, and a journal for taking notes.

See <www.reading.org/publications/IRA_studygroups.html>.

# The Librarian's Link

Librarians throughout the country are discovering the magic and the power of conversations in their school libraries. One of the more exciting programs is called "Library Lunchtime," a program that began 13 years ago at Northeast Elementary School in Ithaca, New York (Baum, 2002). Since the speakers are such a diverse group, the school librarian reviews the ground rules before each session. Students and adults are reminded to raise their hands before speaking and to not get up to empty their lunch trays. If there is more than one reminder to maintain good behavior, the student must leave.

Originally when the Library Lunchtime program began, the librarian issued four passes per class as a way to control the audience size and instill a sense of privilege in attending. For those who sincerely want to attend, that privilege is always extended. The librarian also attempts to match speakers with grade level interests and appropriateness.

For this Library Lunchtime program, the librarian reports that finding speakers has been quite easy. Community members are eager to come and converse about their special areas of expertise or life experiences. Two examples include a Nobel Prize winner in chemistry and a 57-year-old grandmother who was a world-class weight lifter in her age group!

Guests do not necessarily read a book before they speak. The school librarian collects and displays related books so that they are in sight and readily available. Despite the school library's small physical space, suggestions to move Library Lunchtime to a different location within the elementary school have been nixed by the librarian. She asserts that this is a library program and wants students to know that the library is a place where all sorts of interesting and exciting events happen.

# The Principal's Perspective

A few years ago a group of administrators from Baltimore were visiting a school in New York City's District 15. The principal, Tina Volpe, participated in professional development with the Institute for Learning at the University of Pittsburgh on the

Principles of Learning. The focus for professional development for her school for the year was Accountable Talk. Ms. Volpe, the principal, led professional development activities. On the date of this visit, her leadership and understanding of the importance of conversation was not something she just talked about, but something she did.

During this visit, a third grade classroom was observed having a discussion about a chapter book they were reading. The children and teacher obviously were self-conscious because of the visitors, and conversation was not happening naturally. In a supportive way, Ms. Volpe joined the group and facilitated the conversation by using the sentence stems from Accountable Talk. Students began to talk naturally, forgetting the visitors.

Principals who have formed a literacy framework within their schools know the value of sharing with faculty their expectations for conversations. Student-to-student conversations make a noisy, busy classroom. All literacy stakeholders need to be reminded that a quiet, non-participatory classroom does not provide the learning atmosphere for real literacy to happen.

## The Collaboration

Conversations for real literacy occur in schools. Students talk about books. Teachers talk about books. Librarians and principals talk about books. Conversations include personal responses to text. "Personal response is an account of the transaction that occurs between the reader and the text as meaning evolves. Personal response is an essential first step in reading" (Booth and Rowsell, 2002, p. 107).

As principals visit classrooms during literacy instructional times, book talk should be heard. When librarians assist students with selections of reading materials for both pleasure and for assignments, book talk should be heard. As teachers mingle in hallways and meet for morning coffee, book talk should be heard. Literacy leaders in the school assist in the development of literacy conversations by modeling it themselves. Conversation is as much a part of a literacy-focused school as reading and writing.

# Reading the Minds of Others

## References

Almasi, J. (1996). A new view of discussion. In L.B. Gambrell & J.F. Almasi (Eds.). *Lively Discussions! Fostering engaged reading.* Newark, DE: The International Reading Association.

Baum, Karen. (2002). A legend in their own lunchtime. *School Library Journal, 48* (9), 41–47.

Billings, L. & Fitzgerald, J. (2002). Dialogic discussion and the paideia seminar. *American Educational Research Journal, 39* (4), 907–941.

Booth, D. & Rowsell, J. (2002). *The literacy principal: Leading, supporting, assessing reading and writing initiatives.* Ontario, Canada: Pembroke.

Campbell, R. (2001). *Read-alouds with young children.* Newark, DE: The International Reading Association.

Evans, K.S. (2001). *Literature discussion groups in the intermediate grades: Dilemmas and possibilities.* Newark, DE: The International Reading Association.

Fullan, M. (2001). *The new meaning of educational change (3rd ed.).* NY: Teacher's College Press.

Institute for Learning (2001). *Accountable talk: Classroom conversation that works.* Pittsburgh, Pa.: Learning Research and Development Center, University of Pittsburgh. Retrieved September 29, 2003, from <http//:www.instituteforlearning.org>.

Peterson, R. & Eeds, M. (1990). *Grand conversations: Literature groups in action.* NY: Scholastic.

Raphael, T.E. & McMahon, S.I. (1994). Book club: An alternative framework for reading instruction. *The Reading Teacher, 48,* 102–117.

Raphael, T.E., Pardo, L.S., & Highfield, K. (2002). *Book club: A literature-based curriculum (2nd ed.).* Newark, DE: The International Reading Association.

# Chapter 8

# Integrating Reading and Writing for Real Literacy

## An Educator's Voice

"The best literacy instruction should have natural connections for students and be easily integrated."

◆ Elementary teacher and graduate student, Towson University

## Anticipation Questions

*Before reading about ways to integrate reading and writing, consider how reading and writing are important in your life:*

**?** What are ways you use reading and writing in everyday life?
**?** Does reflecting in writing improve what you remember when you read?
**?** How can reading and writing be naturally integrated in schools?

## Exploring the Theory

Harste, Woodward, and Burke (1984) identified eight patterns in children's writing, which appeared universally regardless of the socioeconomic status, race, and sex of the children. The majority of the children were three to six years of age, and the samples of their writings were collected over a six-year period. These were the eight patterns that emerged:

**1** *Organization* — systematic and organized reflections that show personal and social decisions,
**2** *Intentionality* — expectation that written marks are signs that elicit responses,
**3** *Generativeness* — the openness of language that leads to growth,
**4** *Risk-taking* — allowing oneself to become vulnerable,
**5** *Social action* — print generates social and cultural language,
**6** *Context* — language functions only in a social cognitive setting,

**7** *Text* — the basic unit of language, and

**8** *Demonstration* — the display of how something is done.

These eight patterns can also be found in the reading processes of children. The interplay of writing with reading and of reading with writing has led many scholars to view these language events as essentially intertwined.

In real literacy practices, reading and writing often go together. Filling in any form or application requires the integrated interaction of these processes. Researchers investigating the use of reading and writing to support each other have found power in the connections (Langer & Allington, 1992; Tierney & Shanahan, 1991). Recent research cautions that although both processes are stronger in combination, they should be individually taught.

Clay (1998) suggests that writing is the process that young children use to begin to understand the code of our language. For each child this discovery is personal and does not follow a "sequenced curriculum" (p. 133). When a child "reads texts of many kinds" and "write texts of many kinds," "a rich network of connections is being constructed" (p. 137).

Teale and Yokota (2000), while examining historical perspectives on literacy instruction, suggest that "Writing — integrated and separate — is central" (p. 7). For beginning readers, writing is the process that brings phonics and thought together.

The research of Tierney & Shanahan (1991) had a powerful influence on classroom practice, suggesting that different and stronger learning outcomes emerge when the uses of reading and writing are combined. After many years of studying this relationship between reading and writing, Shanahan (1997) realized that reading and writing are closely connected, but they need to be taught as different processes as well as they need to be taught how to be used together.

Reading and writing are both constructive processes. Pearson & Tierney (1984) categorize the roles of reader and of writer as involving similar kinds of knowledge and meaning construction. Cooper (2000, p. 335) suggests that readers and writers actually take on roles. He defined the roles as planner, composer, editor, and monitor, explaining that the same roles are actively involved in both processes. See Figure 8.1 for an overview of these roles.

| The Roles of the Reader and Writer | | |
|---|---|---|
| *PROCESSES* | *READER* | *WRITER* |
| PLANNER | The reader has a purpose for reading. | The writer brainstorms before beginning to write. |
| COMPOSER | As the reader reads, meaning is constantly adjusted. | As the writer writes, words are joined in a continual process. |
| EDITOR | The reader changes his thinking until what was read makes sense. | The writer changes words until the writing says what he wants. |

**Figure 8.1:** Roles of Readers and Writers

Rosenblatt (1978, 1991) was the first to suggest that all readers do not get the same meaning from text. Before her work, reading comprehension/writing connection was considered to be writing answers to specific questions. She changed this practice by rejecting the idea that all readers would have the same answers to questions after they read. Her work proposes that readers have minds of their own and exist in a social context that brings different meanings to what they read. She suggested new thinking about how readers respond to text, emphasizing the transactions among the text, the reader, and the context of the reading activity. She was the first to point out that for reading to be a literate activity, meaning has to play an important role. According to her view, reading of certain texts demanded an "aesthetic" response, where the reader experiences the reading, and reading of other texts demanded an "efferent" response, where the reader remembers information and facts.

Langer (1990) expanded Rosenblatt's theory to include four ways to respond to reading. She explained this process of reading "involves envisionment–building" and used the analogy of "standing in the literature" to explain her theory (p. 812). Envisionment is "what the reader understands at a particular point in time, the questions she has, as well as her hunches about how the piece will unfold" (p. 812). Her "standing in literature" theory describes how readers respond to reading by the following:

■ *Being Out and Stepping In* — the initial understanding stage where the reader grasps  main idea, characters, plot, and setting.
■ *Being In and Moving Through* — the reader connects with prior knowledge and personal experiences, and goes beyond past understandings.

- *Being In and Stepping Out*—the reader uses what is read to reflect on his or her own life.
- *Stepping Out and Objectifying the Experience*—the reader judges the text and relates it to other text experiences.

The theories of Rosenblatt and Langer changed reading/writing connection activities forever. From these theories rose literacy activities that permeate literacy-based classrooms today: quick-writes, readers' response journals, open-ended questions after reading that the writer has to use multiple levels of support to answer, readers' workshop, and writers' workshop.

In a reading workshop, the following occurs:

**1** The teacher teaches a mini lesson (10–20 minutes) on a specific skill or strategy that the students need.
**2** The students choose books to read and apply the strategy.
**3** Students respond to their reading by using some writing techniques.
**4** Students share with classmates (Atwell, 1987, 1998).

In a writing workshop, the following occurs:
**1** The teacher teaches a mini lesson on one of the following: procedure, writing process, qualities of good writing, and editing skills (Fletcher & Portalupi, 2001).
**2** Often, quality children's literature is shared as a model (Harwayne, 1992, 2001).
**3** Children are given large blocks of time to write on topics of their choice (Graves, 1994).
**4** Children share their writing with one another.

Reading and writing are reciprocal practices that require access to quality books and reading materials. The International Reading Association (1999) suggests that the key to many of the reading/writing connected instructional strategies depends on quality school libraries offering children a wide choice of reading materials that they can make connections with and respond to in writing. As children learn to read, they also experiment with writing. All of these experiences are crucial as the students journey towards becoming literate adults who choose to read and write.

# The Practice

As research suggests, writing has to be explicitly taught. In addition, children need designated hours of time each week to practice. Writing time in literacy-based classrooms should mirror what real writers do. The children choose their own topics, ask peers for advice and editing suggestions, and publish their work (Graves, 1994). What they are reading leads to powerful topics and high quality writing. Writing in all subject areas and shared throughout the school provides real literacy contexts for writing to be practiced and valued.

Cambourne's "Conditions for Learning," explained in Chapter 2, guides the teaching of writing in real literacy classrooms. Teachers demonstrate how good writers write by sharing their writing and that of quality children's authors. Immersion, approximation, and engagement set the stage for the largest amount of time spent on writing in the classroom. Children need time to experiment, get support from each other, and think like a writer. Teachers set high expectations for finished products by giving students the responsibility to work through the process at their own pace. At the end of the process, the students share their work and accept responses from their peers.

This process follows a writing workshop model. The teacher begins with a mini lesson centered on what the children's writings indicate they need. The children spend a large block of time writing, conferring, and revising. Each writing session ends with a sharing session where students share finished products or short powerful pieces. Sharing time can also be a time to share small successes or struggles.

Teaching the natural literacy interaction of reading and writing begins with immersion in the works of good writers. Showing children how good writers use the art of writing gives them models upon which to base their own writing.

Teaching good writing can happen in the library as well as the classroom. Collaboration between teachers and librarians enriches this process. Looking at children's writing to understand the needs, planning time to write in the classrooms, and looking at quality writing in the library can help children understand that writing is not just something that you do in school but how literate adults communicate. Examples of children's literature that show how good writers use words to express ideas are the following:

- *A Snow Story* (Leavitt, 1995) is full of wonderful adjectives and rich figurative language.
- *In My Momma's Kitchen* (Nolen, 1999) contains seven short "memories" of the author about events she remembers from her mother's kitchen. This book is a great resource to begin teaching children how to write memoirs.
- An author study on Patricia Polacco, especially using her books, *My Ol' Man* (1995), *Meteor* (1987), *Thank You, Mr. Falker* (1998), and many others that tell stories from her life, is a wonderful connection to begin a memoir-writing project.
- *Tar Beach* (Ringgold, 1991) gives many examples of different types of sentence structure.

In a school focused on literacy, many opportunities to combine reading and writing are naturally infused into every classroom, including the library, art room, and gym. Writing in response to reading gives readers a powerful and tangible transformation of their thoughts about the book. Character cubing, quick writes, response journals, and double entry journals are ways that the reading/writing connection can be incorporated into all parts of the instructional day.

## Character Cubing

**1** Name the book in which the character appeared.
**2** Name three physical characteristics of the character.
**3** Name three personality descriptions of the character.
**4** Tell if you thought the character was a hero/heroine in the book.
**5** Decide if you could relate/identify with the character and name two ways that you could/could not.
**6** Name the character.

The Character Cube combines both an aesthetic and an efferent response to a text. Have a one-dimensional cube drawn on paper. Students will fill in the six sides of the cube before cutting and pasting the cube together. For more interactions, have students leave number six side of the cube empty. Students then find a partner and toss their character cubes to their partner. The partner verbally fills in the number six side of the cube.

## Quick Write

**1** Take a quote out of something the students are going to read.
**2** Put it on an overhead transparency.
**3** Share it on an overhead projector.
**4** Give the students about five minutes to write a response to this short selection.
**5** They can write questions, predictions, or whatever comes into their minds.

This strategy needs to be taught to the students. They begin to write immediately after the prompt and continue to write until the teacher says to stop. The expectation is that all students are writing. Begin quick writes by doing it everyday for the first 10 minutes of class until the students do it automatically. Quick writes force the students to make a connection with the text before reading, motivate them to see if their predictions are right, and involve students in the reading without long discussions.

## Response Journals

**1** Students have a journal for this purpose.
**2** After they read, they respond to the reading by writing.
**3** Lists of prompts or sentence starters help the students choose what to write.

Response journals have become a staple in literacy-based classrooms. Children can respond in journals when reading for pleasure, reading in a book club, or reading an assigned selection. Some teachers collect journals to better understand how their students are thinking and what strategies they are using. Journals also are often shared with peers.

## Double Entry Journals

**1** The journal page is divided in half with a line down the middle of the page.
**2** On the left side, the student writes a quote or a summary of what is read.
**3** On the right side, the student responds to the written quote on the left side.

**Double Entry Journal**

| *Quote or Summary* | *Response* |
| --- | --- |
| *"To be or not to be; that is the question."* | *I often think about this. I am not sure of what I want to do in certain situations.* |

**Figure 8.2:** Double Entry Journal

The double entry journal forces the reader/writer to choose parts of the text to connect with and to reflect on the connection. This journal is effective for book clubs because it helps students to remember passages they want to bring up in discussions.

## Readers' Notebooks

**1** Every child in the school carries a notebook from class to class.
**2** Children write in their notebooks whenever they read something that could be used in their writing. These ideas could be quotes, writing ideas, books to use as models, or words that they like.
**3** A section of the notebook is set aside to record all of the books that they read.
**4** Another section of the notebook is set aside for the books they want to read.

The readers' notebook can be a strategy used throughout the school to integrate reading and writing. The notebooks are either bought or required of all of the children in the school. All teachers are aware of the notebooks and encourage the children to use them whenever they are reading. Small journals, black and white composition books, or homemade journals consisting of construction paper covers and white writing paper could be used. The notebooks need to be small enough that children can carry them all day. This strategy transforms the children's thinking into that of writers who are always thinking about what they are going to be writing next and readers who use their reading to influence writing and thinking.

## Many Real Life Contexts for Reading/Writing Integration

Natural contexts for reading and writing should also be thoughtfully infused throughout the school. Giving children forms in the library, in the school office, in the gym, and in the cafeteria provide practice in real literacy contexts for writing. Putting up large pieces of bulletin board backing paper in the hallways, cafeteria, and library where children can share their ideas and opinions on a subject motivates many children to write and others to read their writings. Imagine a wall of the library with a huge piece of yellow backing paper and the words "Have you read a good book? Tell everyone about it." Imagine a wall of the cafeteria with the words "What is your favorite cafeteria food and why?" Writing becomes fun, and reading each other's writing motivates even the most reluctant reader.

## Information Technology Links

The American Library Association (2003) suggests that information technology provides a natural bridge to "build partnerships for learning." Standards for library media specialists emphasize the importance of teaching children to access information effectively, evaluate the information, synthesize information from many sources, and use this information creatively. The Internet and many software sources supply some of the most motivating reading resources for children of the 21st century. Teaching children to capture the information on note cards, in their readers' notebooks, and on visual organizers provides many opportunities for reading and writing integration in the library. Seeing the roles that authentic writing experiences can play in real literacy produces many wonderful collaborative projects to build partnerships between the library and the classroom. The following projects are examples of collaboration:

■ Teachers initiate a research project in the classroom, and writing time is devoted to the development of the project. In the library, the children use the Internet and other print resources to find out about their topic. The librarian demonstrates in mini lessons ways for students to write down their information (note cards, visual organizers).

■ A project is initiated in the classroom to write a brochure about a place to visit. The brainstorming and writing is done in the classroom. In the library, children are given the opportunity to examine brochures, visit Web sites, and read books about various locations.

■ Mini lessons on how to synthesize the resources into an original context are led by the librarian.

■ Children create a brochure about their school library, using shared writing as a way to practice this type of synthesis. The brochures could be copied and made available for other children in the school to use when visiting the library.

■ Putting together a literary magazine or anthology of writing helps children value one another's writing. Learning the capabilities of word processing and using a scanner, older children put together the literary magazine or anthology from writing submitted by children in the school. As part of this process, the children examine other literary magazines or anthologies. The librarian assists students in writing criteria for submitting and judging writing. Students develop submission forms and acceptance/rejection letters.

■ Using interactive writing, the librarian or teacher guides young children to write one-sentence book reviews after a read-aloud. These reviews are displayed in the library to encourage other children to read books.

Many choices in instructional writing strategies are now part of literacy-based classrooms. Overviews of these strategies follow.

## Mini Lessons
### *Appropriate for All Ages*
Mini lessons are short, focused instructional lessons that teach specific skills. These skills that are taught emerge from careful analysis of the writings of the children. Mini lessons are about 10 minutes, and they never last more than 20 minutes. Often, quality children's literature is used to model how good writers write. For example, a book with good description enhanced by strong verbs shows children how to improve verbs in their writing. In *Verdi* by Janell Cannon (1997), verbs such as "zig-zagged" and "ventured" reveal the power of descriptive writing.

## Interactive Writing
### *Appropriate for Kindergarten and First Grade*
Teachers and children create a sentence to write together. Using chart paper, the children write the sentence. In this writing process, the children are thinking about how the words are spelled, how the letters are formed, how punctuation is used, and how words are placed in a correct way.

A procedure called "sharing the pen" is also used. In sharing the pen the children take turns writing the words on the chart. The other children coach them and give them support.

While one child is writing, the other children have white boards or black-boards and try to create the words themselves so they can be actively engaged in the process. Active engagement is the key to this strategy. Engaged children think about some of the fundamentals of writing: how words are spelled, how sentences are constructed, and how punctuation contributes to the meaning of writing.

## Shared Writing
### *Appropriate for All Elementary Grades*
The teacher and students compose a story, letter, or poem. Children are actively engaged in contributing ideas. Writing is usually done on large pieces of chart paper.

The teacher emphasizes the thinking process of constructing writing, reading for meaning, and concepts of print. He scaffolds when necessary.

Writing pieces are shared in a whole class setting and usually hung on walls, outside halls, and so on. The shared writings are then used as examples for students when they are doing their own writing.

How children receive feedback is also very important. Some ways to give students thoughtful feedback include the following:

■ *Author's Chair*—a special chair is set up in the room where children are invited to sit and share their writing. After a student shares, the listeners give positive and constructive feedback.

■ *Writing Displayed with Constructive Feedback*—students' writing is displayed in the classroom to be enjoyed by members of the class. The teacher's comments on the writing specifically points out what the student did well and suggests the next steps for her as a writer. On finished, published pieces, the comments can be written on sticky notes that are stuck to the paper to value the manuscript. See Figure 8.3 for an example of appropriate comments.

■ *Writing Conferences*—when a child has finished a piece of writing or is at the editing stage, he makes an appointment with the teacher. At the conference the teacher points out the progress the student has made and chooses a few points upon which to coach the student.

■ *Group Critiquing*—gather some small piece of writing from all the students in the class. Put the writing on an overhead transparency. With transparencies on the overhead, guide the children to revise the writing. It is crucial that something is included from all of the students and names are not on the writing. In this way, the students will feel comfortable that no one is singled out.

■ *Sticky Note Critiques*—after the teacher has modeled what constructive comments are, other students in the class can add a sticky note comment on their peers' writing displayed in the classroom.

■ *Instructional Rubrics*—these one- to two-page explanations of what a writing project should entail include the criteria for excellent, average, and poor work (Andrade, 2000). Often, students brainstorm the rubric together. Then, the rubric guides the judging of the project at the editing stage and the final stage. See the following Web sites for examples and guidelines for developing rubrics: <www.rubistar.4teachers.org>, <www.odyssey.on.ca/~elaine.coxon/rubrics.htm>.

---

John,
You did a wonderful job adding powerful verbs to this poem. Next time, try to do the same thing in another type of writing. Since this poem was about snakes, you may want to do research on snakes and write a non-fiction piece.

---

**Figure 8.3:** Comment Example: An example of a teacher's comment that includes what was done well and next steps

# Professional Development Ideas

All educators in the school need to share high expectations for children's writing. Children should be developing an understanding that literate people always write in sentences and use appropriate words in writing to express their thinking. For children to internalize writing as something a literate person does, writing needs to be embedded into all instruction and not just addressed in a one-hour-a-day writing workshop. The Educational Trust in Washington, D.C., works throughout the United States to help teachers understand standards and expectations they should have for students' writing.

The Educational Trust's Standards in Practice Model can change a faculty's understanding of these expectations. The "Trust" suggests, "Students can do no better than the assignments they are given, so those assignments must be demanding, rigorous, and aligned with the highest standards" (2003, p. 1). The Standards in Practice Professional Development Model persuades teachers to develop the kind of assignments that are aligned with high standards.

The model provokes important conversations among all the faculty members about what they ask students to do in writing and what types of student products they accept. Mixing writing teachers, administrators, content area teachers, and the librarian together creates an environment where expectations are confirmed or raised. Higher standards can be developed so that all have an investment in the product. Then, the faculty commits to demanding these standards in writing activities throughout the school. High literacy expectations thus are presented in a unified way to children.

---

## Standards in Practice Professional Development Model

**Step 1:**   Complete the Assignment (10 minutes)
Everyone completes an assignment that has been given to students. By completing an assignment, the educators experience what is being required of the students.

**Step 2:**   Create a Scoring Guide (20 minutes)
The faculty uses the standards, existing school district guidelines, and standardized test expectations to develop a rubric for scoring the assignment. The conversation that results in this phase is very important. Teachers learn a lot about expectations from one another.

**Step 3:**   Score the Student Work (15 minutes)
One assignment is scored by everyone first. Then, the scores are shared and the group discusses the differences until all agree on one score. One assignment can receive anywhere from the lowest to the highest scores. Changes in expectations happen in the discussion of the differences.

**Step 4:**   Study the Results (15 minutes)
How many of the students were able to meet standards?
Was the assignment well designed?
Did the students understand the directions?
This step helps create a shared understanding of ways to create rigorous assignments with higher expectations throughout the whole school curriculum.

> **Step 5:** Plan Changes (15 minutes)
> In this step, the whole school faculty plans together on ways to help all children reach the standards. How can instruction be changed to bring more students up to meeting standards? What kind of assignments would lead to better writing?

The Educational Trust staff lead whole faculty Standards in Practice training by asking everyone to write what education means to them. They share sample student papers and have the participants grade them. Groups talk about their grades in small groups to agree on one group grade. Finally, all of the group grades are compared. Faculties that participate in these development sessions change their thinking about expectations for student writing throughout the school. More information about The Education Trust can be found on their Web site <www.edtrust.org.>.

# The Librarian's Link

Author studies that examine how good writers write are crucial in setting writing standards for children by providing them with good models. The school librarian can be the best person to find these books. Developing a collection of books in the school library that can be used to teach different writing conventions (e.g., strong verbs, rich description) can enrich a school literacy program by infusing quality children's literature into the writing process. Real literacy models lead children to think like writers. Shelley Harwayne's (1992) book, *Lasting Impressions*, suggests many books that could be part of this collection.

Devoting an area of the library to books written by students, staff, and faculty also sets the standard that writing is a literacy practice to be honored. Some printing companies will professionally print and bind student-made books (many have Internet sites). Homemade bindings and laminated covers can also create "published" books. Children can then check out and read books by their peers, principal, and teachers.

Cooperative projects that entail research in the library and writing in the classrooms create curriculum integration and usually produce very strong outcomes. The library has many resources for in depth study that most classrooms lack. Librarians, also, are more knowledgeable about different print sources and are adept with guiding student Internet searches.

# The Principal's Perspective

At Furley Elementary School in Baltimore, Maryland, the principal, Barbara Myers, displays her valuing of quality student writing. At the entrance of the school, the "Principal's Gallery of Quality Writing" welcomes you. On both sides of the hallway are students' writings with comments written on stickies by Ms. Meyers.

Not only is Ms. Meyers honoring the writing, but also she is modeling for the teachers what kinds of comments she expects. She also invites the assistant principal, instructional support teachers, librarian, and content area teachers to set up similar galleries in other parts of the building. Naturally, throughout the building, teachers are putting up their own galleries, too.

To also involve parents in the process, Ms. Meyers calls parents each evening to share with them that their child's work is being exhibited. She explains where the writing is posted and how this piece of writing shows improvement. Then, she invites the parent to come to the school to see what their children have created.

## The Collaboration

Writing, as one of the major components of literacy, needs to be included in all parts of the curriculum and throughout the school. Professional development for faculty and the professional staff needs to start with the faculty examining how they feel about writing and should describe the art of good writing techniques. Writing is then taught in the classroom. It is also used as a cognitive answer to reading in all content areas. Real writing activities, such as filling out forms and forums for stating opinions, can be placed in the school office, library, gym, and cafeteria.

Some school-wide efforts to help children view themselves as writers also promote real literacy. Children have readers' notebooks that they write in all their classes. A book collection for teachers that includes books for authors' study and books to use for writing conventions gives teachers the opportunity to share what good writers do. The library features a special section of books written by children and teachers in the school to celebrate these home-grown authors.

Often when we read in everyday life, writing does follow. This chapter suggested many ways real reading and writing integration happens throughout the school. Reading should lead to writing, and good writing should be read.

## Reading the Minds of Others

### References

American Association of School Librarians (2003). *Information power: Building partnerships for learning.* Retrieved September 29, 2003, from <http://www.ala.org/asslTemplate.cfm?Section=Information_Power&Template=/contenM>.

Andrade, H.G. (2000). Using rubrics to promote thinking and learning. *Educational Leadership* (February), 13–18.

Atwell, N. (1987). *In the middle: Writing, reading and learning with adolescents.* Portsmouth, NH: Heinemann.

Atwell, N. (1998). *In the middle: New understandings about reading and writing with adolescents (2nd ed.).* Upper Montclair, NJ: Boynton/Cook.

Cannon, J. (1997). *Verdi.* New York: Harcourt Brace & Company.

Clay, M.M. (1998). *By different paths to common outcomes.* York, ME: Stenhouse.

Cooper, J.D. (2000). *Literacy: Helping children construct meaning (4th ed.).* Boston, MA: Houghton Mifflin Company.

The Educational Trust (2003). *Standards in practice*. Retrieved May 29, 2003, from
    <http://www.edtrust.org/main/main/sip.asp>.

Fletcher, R. & Portalupi, J. (2001). *Writing Workshop: The Essential Guide*.
    Portsmouth, NH: Heinemann.

Graves, D.H. (1994). *A fresh look at writing*. Portsmouth, NH: Heinemann.

Harste, J., Woodward, V. & Burke, C. (1984). *Language stories and literacy lessons*.
    Portsmouth, NH: Heinemann.

Harwayne, S. (1999). *Going public*. Portsmouth, NH: Heinemann.

Harwayne, S. (1992). *Lasting impressions*. Portsmouth, NH: Heinemann.

Harwayne, S. (2001). *Writing through childhood: Rethinking process and product*.
    Portsmouth, NH: Heinemann.

International Reading Association (1999). *Providing books and other print
    materials for classroom and school libraries*. Newark, DE: The
    International Reading Association.

Langer, J.A. (1990). *Understanding literature. Language Arts, 67*, 812–816.

Langer, J.A. & Allington, R.L. (1992). Curriculum research in writing and
    reading. In P. Jackson (Ed.). *Handbook of research on curriculum*
    (p. 687–725). Old Tappan, NJ: Macmillan.

Leavitt, M.J. (1995). *A snow story*. New York: Simon & Schuster.

Neuman, S., Copple, C., & Bredekamp, S. (2000). *Learning to read and write:
    Developmentally appropriate practices for young children*. Washington,
    DC: National Association for the Education of Young Children.

Nolen, J. (1999). *In my momma's kitchen*. New York: Lothrop, Lee & Shepard
    Books.

Pearson, P.D. & Tierney, R.J. (1984). On becoming a thoughtful reader: Learning to
    read like a writer. In A.C. Purves & O. Niles (Eds.). *Becoming readers in a
    complex society. Eighty-third Yearbook of the National Study of the Science
    of Education* (p. 144–173). Chicago: University of Chicago Press.

Polacco, P. (1987). *Meteor*. New York: G.P. Putnam's Sons.

Polacco, P. (1995). *My ol' man*. New York: Scholastic.

Polacco, P. (1998). *Thank you, Mr. Falker*. New York: Philomel Books.

Ringgold, F. (1991). *Tar beach*. New York: Crown Publishers, Inc.

Rosenblatt, L.M. (1991). Literature — SOS! *Language Arts, 68*, 444–448.

Rosenblatt, L.M. (1978). *The reader, the text, the poem: The transactional theory of
    the literacy work*. Carbondale: Southern Illinois University Press.

Shanahan, T. (1997). Reading-writing relationships, thematic units, inquiry learning
    in pursuit of effective integrated literacy instruction. *Reading Teacher, 51*
    (1), 12–19.

Teale, W.H. & Yokota, J. (2000). Beginning reading and writing: Perspectives on
    instruction. In D.S. Strickland & L.M. Morrow (Eds.). *Beginning Reading
    and Writing*, 3–21. NY: Teachers' College Press.

Tierney, R.J. & Shanahan, T. (1991). Research on the reading-writing relationship:
    Interactions, transactions, and outcomes. In R. Barr, M.L. Kamil, P.B.
    Mosenthal, & P.D. Pearson (Eds.). *Handbook of reading research, Volume II*,
    (p. 246–280). White Plains, NY: Longman.

# Chapter 9

# Natural Assessment in Real Literacy

## An Educator's Voice

"I love to teach. I do not mind hard work or large time demands. What I do resent greatly is the expenditure of great amounts of time (my students' as well as mine) coupled with their and my best efforts only to have the children fall short of what the system expects them to achieve."

A Second Grade Teacher in a Low-Achieving Baltimore City School, Maryland

## Anticipation Questions

*The new federal legislation,* No Child Left Behind *(2003), dictates serious consideration of assessment data to make school-based decisions. Therefore, a school-wide focus and understanding of the role assessment plays in literacy instruction are crucial for following the federal guidelines. This understanding is equally important for real literacy development in a school. Begin this exploration by examining existing views of assessment.*

- What do we mean by assessment that drives instruction?
- Why do classroom observations of real literacy events lead to increased student achievement?
- What is the relationship between standardized tests and natural classroom assessments?
- How can natural assessments be embedded into all literacy instruction?

## Exploring the Theory

Both early childhood and reading policymakers strongly advocate for assessments that are authentic, that drive instruction, and that are developmentally appropriate (Neuman, Copple, & Bredekamp, 2000; IRA, 1991, 1999). The more formal, standardized tests (e.g., Comprehensive Test of Basic Skills, Iowa Test of Basic Skills) yield useful data for comparing programs, curricula, schools, districts, and states. They produce good quantitative data on populations of students, but often do not "reflect the complexity of reading" (IRA, 1999). However, the use of natural, authentic assessments that emphasize real literacy tasks provides an authentic demonstration of what children know and what they need to learn.

Focusing on authentic literacy tasks helps educators understand true literacy achievement of their students and thus guides them continually on this path. Often, focusing on high-stakes testing only results in teacher frustration and does little to move children closer to real literacy (IRA, 1999). Achievement data from standardized assessments only give a snapshot of how students do on isolated reading tasks in contrast to the bigger picture of the students' strengths and needs evolved from naturalistic assessments.

Natural assessments are designed to guide instruction. They give immediate information about a student's literacy capabilities and current achievements. Comparing students' results to standards and school system curriculum requirements, instruction can be tailored to meet students' needs from these assessments.

Jett-Simpson & Leslie (1997, p. 12) suggest eight characteristics of authentic assessments designed to guide instruction:

- Used to assess the effect of particular instruction,
- Materials and procedures come from classrooms, thus will vary,
- Can be given at any time,
- Immediate feedback possible because teachers score them,
- Interpreted in view of other measures,
- Results subject to change through immediate instruction, and
- Major use is within the classroom.

Natural, authentic assessments are used every day as a teacher constantly readjusts the scaffolding to allow her students to gain independence and self-efficiency with each new literacy skill and strategy. The teacher looks at work samples, collects finished work, has students do self-evaluations, looks at student journals, uses checklists, and takes anecdotal records (Armbruster & Osborn, 2002).

Clay (1998, p. 207) suggests that the most important assessment of children's literacy achievement is to allow them to "conduct the orchestra" by themselves. Let children read, talk about the reading, and share with the teacher what is happening in their brain when they read. She further suggests that we close the doors on high literacy achievement when we use only prescribed assessment practices. The teacher needs to know where the child is and teach the child to go further.

The Running Record designed by Clay (1993) was designed to capture how the student is actually reading. Using real children's books, the child reads and the teacher takes down a combination of checks for words read correctly and snapshots of the errors made. The errors are recorded using a set of universal symbols so that others, in addition to the recorder, can understand what the student is doing when they read. The errors, which are called "miscues," then are analyzed to give the teacher clues to what strategies the child uses.

The child then retells the story. The teacher listens to see whether the student is learning the concept of literary forms (setting, character, theme), what connections are made to the text, whether the child understands underlying meanings, and whether the child retells the story in the sequence it was presented by the author (beginning, middle, and end). As the teacher is listening to this retelling, he may be taking written notes, using a retelling grid or a story outline.

The following is an example of a retelling grid:

|  | Yes | No | Comments |
|---|---|---|---|
| Setting<br>Characters<br>Plot/Theme<br>Beginning<br>Middle<br>End<br>Inferences |  |  |  |

Points are awarded to each section so a score can be found. Often, too, event episodes could be listed.

If the student hesitates in the retelling, the teacher may ask questions. This retelling then becomes an aided one, with the teacher helping to focus the student's remembrance of the sequence in the story.

These assessments are natural and authentic because they flow from the story, and they represent student understanding of the concept being taught. In contrast, a more formalized, standardized assessment of knowledge of literary forms would entail a multiple-choice test with each student reading independently to conclude with answers bubbled in on a scantron sheet. These assessments are usually scored in a district or statewide process that takes six to nine months and do not yield "enough information to make important instructional decisions" (IRA, 1999, p. 5). The immediacy of the feedback on the student's achievement in natural assessments makes them more effective to guide further student instruction.

Motivation, interest, and attitude are also important elements that influence students' real literacy (Gambrell, Palmer, Codling & Mazzoni, 1996). Surveys, motivation interviews, and questionnaires help the teacher construct a better understanding of the child as a reader (Armbruster & Osborn, 2002). Self-evaluation checklists and reflections assess the students' understanding of themselves as readers, thus providing important opportunities for the teacher to connect the learning to the students' real literacy needs (Miller, 1995).

Listed here are several kinds of natural, authentic assessments that are used for real literacy assessment (Also see Figure 9.1, Components of Literacy Assessment):

- **Anecdotal Records** — Brief, written notes are made by a teacher based on observations of the student's literacy actions.
- **Checklists** — written assessments that have lists of literacy abilities or behaviors that a teacher can check as present, sometimes present, or not present in a child. Checklists can be teacher-made and designed for specific purposes.

- **_Interest Inventories and Attitude Surveys_**—lists of questions (and sometimes illustrations) capture in a quick way what children like to read and how they feel about themselves as readers.
- **_Journals_**—students write responses to reading.
- **_Learning Logs_**—students reflect in writing on what they are learning.
- **_Portfolios_**—an organized collection of many of the above assessments that show the growth over time of students' literacy skills are included in portfolios.
- **_Primary Trait Evaluations_**—the rubrics combine characteristics of both holistic scoring and analytical scoring. The criteria for the analytical scoring include a list of only a few, selected items, and the piece of writing is evaluated holistically on this small set of criteria (Bratcher, 1994, p. 61).
- **_Projects_**—authentic activities done in conjunction with reading. Could be little books, book reports, posters, brochures, or art. They are analyzed using a rubric that lists the competencies that are being assessed.
- **_Retellings_**—the teacher listens as a student retells a story and captures the main story elements, theme, strategies used, and implied meanings understood. Sometimes teachers use a retelling protocol or guide to determine if all areas have been covered.
- **_Running Records_**—standardized procedures designed by Clay (1993) to capture children's miscues and strategies when reading. The children actually read trade books that are on their reading level, and the teacher takes notes using set procedures for recording.
- **_Work Samples_**—daily assignments and pieces of student writing often give the teacher an immediate window into how the student is learning what is taught.
- **_Written Vocabulary Test_**—this assessment was designed by Clay (1993) to capture young children's knowledge of how words work. Children are asked to write all the words they know in a 10-minute time period. The words are analyzed to determine how much the student knows about words. For example, the child who writes a whole list of words that rhyme is beginning to realize how words have similar parts.

# The Practice

The United States Department of Education (2003) mandate _No Child Left Behind_ connects all school funding to student achievement. School faculties are charged with collaborating to find ways to track the progress of all students in their schools. State departments of education must track progress using standardized tests that have results that are returned to the schools before the beginning of the next school year. These results then are used to enhance instruction to improve the achievement of all students regardless of ethnicity, race, or gender.

Student achievement is the job of not only the classroom teacher but the whole faculty. Faculties review test data together, choose ways to improve the achievement of all children in the school, and decide on ways to address the needs of the lowest achieving children. Once plans are in place to improve literacy instruction, how to assess student progress towards these goals during the year has to

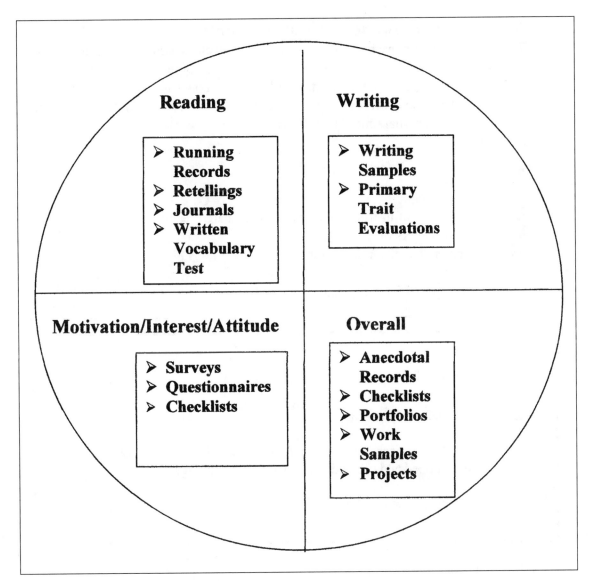

**Figure 9.1:** Components of Literacy Assessment

be decided. If schools depend only on standardized assessment, children not achieving during the school year will be behind before the next testing report comes back.

The International Reading Association suggests that informal, authentic assessment provides educators with immediate feedback on the progress and needs of children (1999, 1991). Many of these assessments were explained in the previous section of this chapter. They provide many opportunities to look at the literacy activities of children through many different lenses.

These authentic observations of student progress can be administered by other literacy leaders as well as by classroom teachers. In a literacy-focused school, collaboration among different faculty allows a clearer picture of the child to emerge. An important key to achievement, which is demonstrated on standardized tests and in real literacy settings, is gradual release of responsibility, as outlined in Chapter 2 of this book. Assessment of independent engagement often is more effective outside the classroom than in the classroom under the teacher's direction.

## Across School Authentic Assessments

The librarian, the art teacher, and the principal, as well as a classroom teacher, could do anecdotal records of student use of literacy. Anecdotal records are quick notes taken when observing children. A standard 3"-by-5" note card that is clipped to a clipboard allows the observer to write efficient notes on how the child is using literacy during instructional time. The following are five necessary components of an anecdotal record:

**1** Date,

**2** Name of student,

**3** Name and time of instruction, (for example, shared reading time, 9–9:20 a.m.),

**4** Literacy behaviors of the student, and

**5** Texts that are handled/read/skimmed.

See Figure 9.2 for an example.

4/9/03
Patience Jones

Language Arts Block, 9:15 to 9:35

Tracking text with her finger. Much more focused than the last time I observed. Three times she stopped and broke down a word with her finger.

Text: *The Very Hungry Caterpillar*

**Figure 9.2:** Sample Anecdotal Record

Response logs, learning logs, presentations, demonstrations, and projects can be used in any class in the school to understand how children have internalized and demonstrated reading and writing. Art projects that include examining books and written reflection on the product become literacy projects. Gym demonstrations that involve following written directions and collaboration with peers become literacy demonstrations. Interdisciplinary projects in social studies and science involving visual presentation, collaboration, and reading can be analyzed for literacy proficiency. Written logs in any class in response to reading or learning provide another means to analyze how children are progressing on literacy outcomes.

## Running Records

Another important authentic assessment for real literacy is a running record (Clay, 2000, 1993; Fountas & Pinnell, 1996). Running records tell teachers how well a child is able to process print. It is like an open window into a child's mind as she attempts to make meaning from those crazy little symbols on the page. In the CEO's District of Baltimore City (a district consisting of the nine lowest achieving schools in the state), administrators, content area teachers, and librarians all assist daily in the language arts block by completing running records. This assessment provides both an opportunity for children to read to adults and a process to capture the reading behaviors.

To do a running record, the teacher records with established symbols what a child is doing when he reads. Running records are usually done on beginning readers or struggling readers to analyze their attempts at attacking text to determine their needs for instruction. See Figure 9.3 for an example of a running record.

## How to Do a Running Record
The basic steps in using a running record on a beginning reader are the following:

- Choose a text on the student's reading level (Fountas & Pinnell, 1998) that you are confident that she will be able to read with ease.
- Read the text yourself so that you are familiar with the story.
- Familiarize yourself with the standard running record notations. Keep a list of the symbols next to you until your comfort level with the notations has been reached.
- Put student and text information at the top of the page.
- Ask the student to read the story aloud explaining that you will be making notes while he is reading.
- As the student reads, use the running record notations for every word that the student reads. If you are uncertain, make a quick ? and continue with the markings.
- Make a notation for everything that the student says. Running records become easier with practice.

*A Quick Tip: Fold a piece of paper in half or use a stenographer pad that has a line down the middle of each sheet. On the left side, take the record; on the right side, analyze it.*

To analyze a running record, the teacher puts the initials MSV on the right side of the record. For each error, the teacher circles whether the error is meaningful (M), structural (S), or visual (V), also called graphic mistakes. Percentages are computed to understand which of these cueing systems the child uses when making errors.

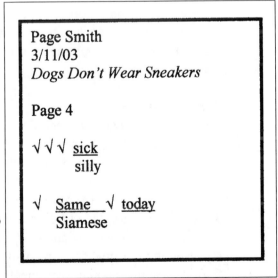

**Figure 9.3:** A Sample Running Record

For more information on taking or recording running records, refer to *Running Records for Classroom Teachers* (Clay, 2000). This resource provides explicit directions, forms, and guidelines for analysis of running records.

## Retelling

Additionally, after the running record is taken, the child retells the story. Retellings clarify whether the child understands what was read. The teacher notes whether the child can sequence the events of the story, provide story elements (characters, setting, etc.), and whether any inferences were made. Sometimes further questions are asked.

### *A useful resource for retelling:*

*Alternative Assessment Techniques for Reading & Writing* (Miller, 1995). The Center of Applied Research (p. 80–122) provides checklists and guidelines to evaluate retellings for different grade levels.

# Professional Development Ideas

For years and years, teachers have used natural assessments. Many excellent teachers observed their students' oral reading, noting their degree of fluency, their attempts to self-correct any miscoded words, and their constant use of the illustrations to help give meaning of the text. Today, these informal assessments have been renamed and tucked away under the broad quilt of natural assessments.

## Theory Share:

*Testing Miss Malarkey* by Judy Finchler (2000) provides a great resource to read aloud at the beginning of professional development on assessment. This humorous story about outrageous activities that go on in a school before the state standardized tests are given provides a grand stage upon which to begin faculty growth. Many of the activities of Miss Malarkey and of the faculty of her school (feeding children fish because it is brain food is an example) bring laughter, but also emphasize how foolish it is to spend student time on isolated tasks to improve student achievement on state tests. Discussion time after this book reveals many insights and reflections on state testing programs.

## The Practice:

There are several paths for faculties to choose to learn more about natural assessments. Some activities that promote important conversations and sharing about informal assessments include the following:

- Designing grade level rubrics for writing pieces,
- Vertical (across grade level) curriculum planning to allow smooth transitions for expectations in writing and reading as students progress from year to year,
- Designing informal assessments together,
- Administering similar instruments across grade levels and discussing results, and
- Practicing taking and analyzing running records.

A good resource for introducing educators to running records is *Teaching the Structural Reading Observation: Step-by-Step Procedures & Materials for Trained Teachers to In-Service Staff* (Kuoni & Colwell, 1998). This resource includes instructions on how to introduce all the running record procedures and a practice audiotape to give teachers a group experience of trying them.

# The Librarian's Link

Research suggests that motivation and interest contribute to children's reading achievement (Gambrell, Palmer, Codling & Mazzoni, 1999). Often, with so many assessments being done in the classrooms, teachers do not have time to assess motivation and interest in reading and literacy. Unfortunately, without an understanding of what will spark literacy interest in a child, teachers might leave children behind.

Librarians have always realized the important connection between reading interests and attitudes of children to literacy development. Through informal conversations and observations, they assess what will motivate children to read. In a literacy-focused school, librarians could formalize this process and guide all educators in the school to understand how motivation, interest, and attitudes impact children's literacy habits.

Attitude surveys, self-evaluation checklists, and motivation interviews provide another snapshot to help the educators in the school understand the needs of the students. *The Motivation to Read Profile* (Gambrell, Palmer, Codling, & Mazzoni, 1996) provides a paper-and-pencil survey that takes about 15 minutes to administer and a personal interview instrument to help understand how students see themselves as readers. *The Elementary Reading Surveys* (McKenna & Kear, 1990) use little happy and sad Garfield figures for young children to choose how they feel about different reading and writing activities. Both of these are available in *Reading assessment: Principles and practices for elementary teachers* (Barrentine, 1999). This resource and *Alternative Assessment Techniques for Reading and Writing* (Miller, 1995) include numerous self-evaluation and survey instruments that can be utilized to understand the literacy skills of all the children.

An informal interest and attitude survey might include the following open-ended questions:

When I read, I _____ .

I like to read books about _____ .

I am happy when I read _____ .

I wish I could read _____ .

Whether using a more formal survey, interview, or an informal project using the above sentence starters, librarians could capture this crucial information about student motivation and interest to share with classroom teachers, administrators, and content area teachers. This sharing could be as simple as developing a folder or binder for each class of children and giving it to all faculty who interact with those children. Advice on how to utilize books in the school library to meet the interests of all of the children naturally follows. Reading motivation programs that are often organized by librarians can now be more focused on meeting individual students' needs.

## The Principal's Perspective

How do principals lead faculties to understand assessment data? One of the six standards developed by the National Association for the Elementary School Principal as exemplary standards for what principals should know and be able to do concerns the use of assessment data (NAESP, 1999). In a study by Pitcher, Mackey, and Decman (2003), the researchers analyzed how four elementary school principals used assessment data and how it affected student achievement. Two of the principals took hard looks at their school literacy programs in their analysis of the data and shared the results with faculty. The one with the highest increase in scores the following year used this analysis to change the school program to a balanced literacy approach, providing faculty with materials and professional development. (Reading scores increased 20 points, which was maintained for two years afterwards.) The other principal added a literacy-based afternoon program, which also showed some (but not as high) increase in scores the next year. The other two schools focused on programs or testing strategies with little increases in scores.

The principal can empower his teachers by sharing the school standardized tests scores and encouraging the faculty to use the data to improve literacy instruction throughout the school. Conversations about yearlong efforts by all parts of the faculty inspire total faculty buy-in. Often, faculty members realize the problems in curriculum that must be addressed to meet all students' academic needs. Honest conversations and real literacy efforts can make a difference.

The principal's daily classroom visits encourage all literacy leaders in the school to consider the literacy needs of all children. Some important questions that all literacy leaders can ask include the following:

■ What level is this child reading on? Can I see his latest running record?
■ How does this child view herself as a reader?
■ Can I see John's last writing sample?
■ What is she interested in reading?

## The Collaboration

Literacy assessment is the job of the whole faculty in a literacy-based school. How children use literacy in every subject area and throughout the school demonstrates true mastery. Professional collaboration for literacy mastery begins with analyzing standardized assessment results to discover program strengths and needs. Next, the data are analyzed to determine which children are achieving and which are being left behind. All of the literacy leaders within the school faculty then plan literacy programs, curricula, and instructional strategies that meet the federal mandate to "Leave No Child Behind."

Including data that are derived from informal literacy assessments is essential for producing effective and developmentally appropriate instruction for each child. Faculty conversations on the literacy strengths and needs of each child build stronger professional bonds. All literacy leaders then plan to meet students' strengths and needs. The cycle of continuous assessment judges how successful these plans are for all children.

# Reading the Minds of Others

## References

Armbruster, B. and Osborn, J.H. (2002). *Reading instruction and assessment: Understanding the IRA standards*. Boston: Allyn and Bacon.

Author. (2001). *Leading learning communities: NAESP standards for what principals know and should be able to do*. Alexandria, VA: National Association of Elementary School Principals.

Barrentine, S.J. (1999). *Reading assessment: Principles and practices for elementary teachers*. Newark, DE: International Reading Association.

Bratcher, S. (1994). *Evaluating children's writing: A handbook of communication choices for classroom teachers*. New York: St. Martin's Press.

Clay, M. (1993). *An observation survey of early literacy achievement*. Portsmouth, NH: Heinemann.

Clay, M. (1998). *By different paths to common outcomes*. York, MA: Stenhouse.

Clay, M. (2000). *Running records for classroom teachers*. Portsmouth, NH: Heinemann.

Finchler, J. (2000). *Testing Miss Malarkey*. New York: Walker and Company.

Fountas, I. & Pinnell, G.S. (1999). *Matching books to readers: Using leveled books in guided reading, K–3*. Portsmouth, NH: Heinemann.

Gambrell, L.B., Palmer, B.M., Codling, R.M., & Mazzoni, S.A. (1999). Assessing motivation to read. In Barrentine, S.J. (Ed.) (1999). *Reading assessment: principles and practices for elementary teachers*. Newark, DE: International Reading Association.

Jett-Simpson, M. & Leslie, L. (1997). *Authentic literacy assessment: An ecological approach*. New York: Longman.

International Reading Association (IRA, 1999). *High-stake assessments in reading: A position statement of the International Reading Association*. Newark, DE: The International Reading Association. Retrieved May 26, 2003 from <http://www.reading.org/positions/lit_assess.html>.

International Reading Association (IRA, 1991). *On literacy assessment: A board resolution*. Newark, DE: The International Reading Association. Retrieved May 26, 2003, from <http://www.reading.org/positions/high_stakes.html>.

Kerr, D.J., Coffman, G.A., McKenna, M.C., & Ambrosio, A.L. (2000). Measuring attitude toward writing: A new tool for teachers. *The Reading Teacher, 54* (1), 10–23.

Kuoni, J. & Colwell, L. (1998). *Teaching the structured reading observation: Step-by-step procedures & materials for trained teachers to in-service staff.* Lincoln City, OR: The Literacy Partnership.

McKenna, M.C., & Kear, D.J. (1990). Measuring attitude toward reading: A new tool for teachers. *The Reading Teacher* (May), 626–639.

McLaughlin, M. & Allen, M.B. (2001). *Guided comprehension: A teaching model for grades 3–8.* Newark, DE: The International Reading Association.

McLaughlin, M. (2003). *Guided comprehension in the primary grades.* Newark, DE: The International Reading Association.

Miller, W.H. (1995). *Alternative assessment techniques for reading and writing.* West Nyack, NY: The Center for Applied Research in Education.

Neuman, S., Copple, C., & Bredekamp, S. (2000). *Learning to read and write: Developmentally appropriate practices for young children.* Washington, DC: National Association for the Education of Young Children.

Pitcher, S., Mackey, B., & Decman, J. (2003). *Taking the lead: How elementary principals influence literacy programs.* Presentation at the Ethnographic and Qualitative Research in Education Annual Conference, Pittsburgh, PA.

Puckett, M.B. & Black, J. (2000). *Authentic assessment of the young child: Celebrating development and learning (2nd ed.).* Upper Saddle River, New Jersey: Merrill.

United States Department of Education (2003). *No child left behind.* Retrieved May 30, 2003, from <http://www.nclb.gov>.

# Subject/Source Index